International Business Management:
A Conceptual Framework

McGraw-Hill Series in International Business
Franklin R. Root, Consulting Editor

Fayerweather: **International Business Management:**
A Conceptual Framework

International Business Management:
A Conceptual Framework

John Fayerweather
Professor of International Business
Graduate School of Business Administration
New York University

McGraw-Hill Book Company

New York
St. Louis
San Francisco
London
Sydney
Toronto
Mexico
Panama

International Business Management:
A Conceptual Framework

Library of Congress Catalog Card Number 69-12259

1 2 3 4 5 6 7 8 9 0 V B V B 7 5 4 3 2 1 0 6 9 8

To Charlie

Editor's Foreword

This book is the first in the McGraw-Hill series in international business. The purpose of the series is to offer educators, students, and executives an ordered set of concise, authoritative studies on the fundamental aspects of international business management and its multinational environment. Each book will complement other texts in the series, and collectively they are intended to cover the full scope of international business. Books now in the writing stage include *The Economics of International Business, Government and International Business, International Marketing Management, International Financial Management,* and *International Business Policy.*

International business is a youthful, exuberant field of study. Before World War II the characteristic response of American companies to market opportunities abroad was via direct export from home-based plants. Although direct exports remain important, the most dynamic form of international business today is the transfer of management, technology, and capital via direct investment in foreign economies. A new business organization—the multinational corporation—has come to the fore, and it now sets the pace for international business throughout the world.

With the advent of the multinational company, the study of international business has exploded in all directions. The full range of top management and business functions with all their many interactions with the economic, political, and cultural aspects of a complex, changing international environment is now grist for the educator's mill. There is a crying need, therefore, for a conceptual framework that helps us relate the many seemingly disparate elements of international business into a comprehensive, meaningful whole.

This is the task that Professor Fayerweather has set for himself in this book. Focusing on the unique role of the multinational company as an international transmitter of resources (in particular, skills of many kinds) and as a change agent, he explores the complementary and conflict relations between host societies and international business. From this analysis, Professor Fayerweather then draws out the implications for global business strategy, organization, and administration. All this is done within a conceptual framework that comes to life in analytical constructs, such as the power-balance approach, that carry both a behavioral and normative significance for a broad span of international business activity. Without pretension, Professor Fayerweather has indeed discharged his task. I can think of no better introduction to the exciting world of international business.

Franklin R. Root
Consulting Editor
Wharton School of Finance and Commerce
University of Pennsylvania

Preface

Perhaps the clearest trend in business education over recent years has been the shift from pragmatic and descriptive material toward conceptual and theoretical approaches. The inclination of scholars to seek out principles and generalizations has doubtless supported this process. But basically its origins are eminently practical. The immense increase in the size and complexity of modern business has forced it upon us. It provides ever greater opportunities and rewards for those whose approaches to business management have broad applicability and who focus on the fundamentals of the business process.

The logics of this trend are as strong in international business as in any other phase of business. The variety among countries, types of business operations, and other facets of international business is so great that the strictly pragmatic or descriptive approaches to achieving competence in the field are cumbersome and unproductive. The value of developing fundamental concepts of broad utility is readily apparent. Unfortunately, international business study is very young. There has scarcely been time to develop such concepts, especially as the research which should underlie them is extremely thin. Yet the need is there, and if international business study is to keep pace with the general trend of business studies and meet the challenges of its own subject matter, conceptual approaches must evolve rapidly.

These reflections put the present book in perspective. It is an attempt to meet an apparent need. Its contents have evolved out of my experience with courses in international business management in three business schools. In these courses I have always found it essential to bring reality to instruction by the use of cases and factual background. But early in my experience it became apparent that some framework to present the operational problems of the international firm more systematically was needed, and from that need emerged my first text, *Management of International Operations*. In due course, I found even this material too variegated and unsystematic to provide fundamental guidance in analysis of international business problems. Thus, my remarks in classes evolved gradually toward defining the limited number of basic themes which recurred regularly in our studies and then to the formulation of a comprehensive blending of the themes into the conceptual framework presented in this book.

As the foregoing suggests, I owe my greatest debt in the conception of the book to my students. The pressure to stay ahead of them and provide them with meaningful guidance has been a powerful motivation. I cannot list all those whose ideas have helped me. Many of them are credited directly in footnotes. A few deserve special note. I owe a particular debt to Richard D. Robinson, in part for the useful comments which he made on my overall scheme, but mostly for the many thoughtful insights which he has contributed as an intellectual leader in the field over the years. More immediately, I am most appreciative of the many helpful comments made by Franklin Root, the editor of this series, and by Arthur Stonehill, who also read the full manuscript. My thanks go also to Mrs. Sophie Karschmidt and Mrs. Mary Jo Leipzig, who typed the manuscript. Finally, there is that special debt which an author owes to the tolerance and encouragement he receives from his family while he pursues the time-consuming, preoccupying task of creating a book.

John Fayerweather

Contents

International Business Management:
A Conceptual Framework

Chapter One
Introduction and Overview

International business, in one sense, is thousands of years old, extending back beyond the Phoenicians to the early traders of primitive times. But in the current sense of a large number of corporations with interrelated production and sales operations located around the world, it is a very recent phenomenon which emerged only in the 1950s. It is not surprising, therefore, that we are at an early stage in trying to formulate a systematic approach to the problems of international business management. The objective of this book is to contribute in that direction by presenting a conceptual framework within which international business problems may be systematically analyzed on the basis of the environmental and corporate variables which affect them.

THE EVOLUTION
OF INTERNATIONAL BUSINESS LITERATURE

The literature of international business to date has largely fallen into two categories: operational detail and functional practice and policy. The *operational detail* material deals with the tremendous volume of specific facts which affect business and which vary in all manner of ways in enterprises which span the globe—export documentation, rates of interest, how people greet each other, regulations on employment of expatriates, and a whole host of other individual aspects of business. Literature of this sort appeared rather quickly because the accumulation of facts is not complicated and there is an urgency of demand for concrete information by businessmen confronted with immediate problems. But in the development of basic competence for international business management, this category of literature is of only limited value. One cannot hope to master all the facts about each particular phase of business and all the countries, so the study of individual situations is useful in this context only for illustrative purposes and as raw material for developing higher levels of analysis.

Approaching the field at the *functional policy and practice* level is more rewarding. One can find certain recurring patterns of environmental conditions and management responses which contribute to capacity to manage international enterprises. For example, in the consideration of personnel management abroad, one finds similar characteristics in such elements as paternalism, wage levels, and skill appearing with sufficient frequency, so that certain ways of thinking and general personnel policies may be applied in many countries. Refinement to fit the operational details of each country is ultimately necessary, but the general international functional skill is effective. Likewise, there are recurring experiences in the handling of personnel sent to overseas posts in such matters as cost-of-living allowances and rotation of assignments from which general guidelines may be evolved. Thus one can acquire competence as an *international* personnel manager, which is broader than personnel competence in a specific foreign country and distinctly different from competence in domestic personnel management. The literature at this level has already grown to impressive proportions with contributions from both practitioners and scholars drawn from the business experience accumulated in the post-World War II era.

For a great many purposes the functional literature is reasonably adequate, serving, for example, the domestic marketing manager who must adapt to a new assignment, including international responsibility or the professor wishing to include an international component in a course in personnel management. However, to more thoughtful people both in management and in academic circles, this is still not enough. They look for something more fundamental, a conceptual base which will comprehend the international components of all the functional fields, a synthesis of what international business management is as an entity unto itself, not just as an extension in different forms of each functional field. This situation is related to that of *management,* which cuts across the

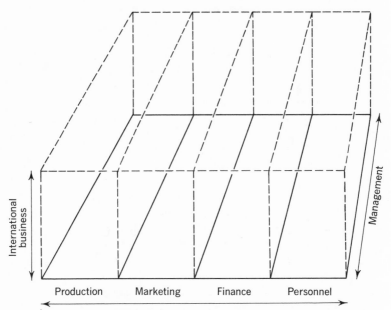

Figure 1.1   The relation of international business to the traditional business fields.

functional fields of production, marketing, etc., contributing skills useful to each. But it is a different order of problem because management has a set of specific operational practices—organization, planning, and the like—which can fairly readily be isolated as observable activities. They are thus properly viewed as an additional functional field in the same plane as the others (Figure 1.1).

The international aspect is of another order, however, lying in a different dimension beyond the domestic phases of the traditional functional fields. The observable activities in this dimension are not distinguishable from similar domestic activities. Planning an advertising program for a group of subsidiaries in the European Common Market has, for example, all the basic characteristics of the same task for a U.S. operation. What differs is that at practically every stage, variations in external factors plus some internal differences attributable to the global character of the business have to be applied. The distinguishing characteristics of the international component are not therefore in the nature of a distinct body of functionally determinable practices and concepts but rather something most intimately related to the external variables found in the cultural, economic, social, and political environments within which international business must be conducted.

The literature at this level is still extremely slim. There have been a few valuable contributions to which specific reference will be made at appropriate points in this book. But they are as yet partial or preliminary in nature, as the essential conceptual features of international business are just emerging from both research studies and syntheses of the literature of the functional international fields.

It is into this relative vacuum that the present book is pointed. It is an attempt to present a comprehensive conceptual approach which will be applicable to *all* the functional fields. The essence of a conceptual framework for the analysis of a particular system of business activities is the development of a set of relationships which are consistent with the internal character of the system and with its environment and which are broad enough in character so that all subordinate questions relevant to the system can be analyzed within the framework. To meet these criteria, we need for international business a framework which will be consistent both with the observed characteristics of international business operations and with the nature of the geographic, political, economic, social, and cultural relations between nations and which will provide basic guidance for analysis of the distinctively *international* aspects of all types of business problems. This is clearly a challenging task and, as with any pioneer effort, there is little expectation that the result will be the last word on the subject. Rather the objective is hopefully to make a useful step ahead by testing the feasibility of constructing such a comprehensive conceptual framework and to give an incentive to others to try further approaches in this direction. In the chapters which follow, the components of the conceptual framework will be spelled out in full. To give the reader a preliminary overview of the territory to be explored, the components will be outlined briefly here, indicating their nature and a sampling of the conclusions toward which they lead.

THE CONCEPTUAL FRAMEWORK

The starting point for the conceptual framework is a definition of international business. Although one can construct quite elaborate definitions of international business, it would appear to have only one central distinguishing characteristic—it is business involving two or more nations. Thus concepts unique to international business must stem directly from business processes intersected in some way by national borders. Although the presence of national borders in the conventional political and geographic sense is the basis for this definition, we must use a more flexible concept of the term *national border* to relate it meaningfully to international business processes. The points at which significantly *internation contact* occurs range geographically from purchase by an Italian importer from a U.S. manufacturer in his plant in the middle of the United States to a French engineer supervising a worker in a Moroccan mine. Likewise, the impact of the intervention of national borders may be felt at two or more points in a continuous business process. For example, the relationships between a managing director of a British firm and an Englishman running its subsidiary in Brazil and between the latter and a Brazilian subordinate are both substantially affected by the intervention of national borders. National border is therefore used in this book to mean the border or contact line between people, companies, and activities which are distinguished from each other for reasons which have their initial origin in the presence of national borders in the conventional sense.

Focusing on the national-border element, we may identify two types of processes which are central to the conceptual framework as shown in Figure 1.2. First, we have those business processes (number 1 in Figure 1.2) which pass through national borders—shipments of goods, transfers of funds, movement of people, and so forth. All these processes are essentially economic transactions in which resources from one nation are transmitted in exchange for resources from another. Second, there are the interactions of a multinational firm with the host society (number 2 in

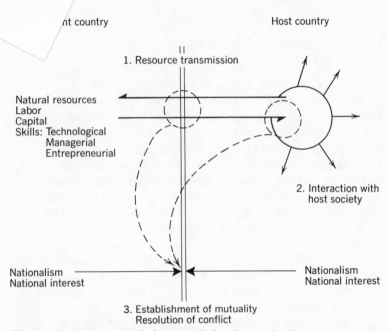

Figure 1.2 A conceptual framework for international business: relationships with single nations.

Figure 1.2). These may in a sense be considered a continuation of the first category as they involve the implementation of the processes of transmission of resources. However, it is conceptually useful to separate the cross-border transmission process and the subsequent processes of interaction with the host society. The differing characteristics of each country *as such* are not included in this phase. They compose an important area of study pursued in the rapidly emerging field of comparative business and in area studies. But they are not properly part of international business because they focus on business processes involving only one country at a time. Thus we are concerned here only with the interaction between the host society and companies which have ties outside the country.

Having defined international business in this way, we readily observe that the key processes are not unique unto themselves. They are rather the business phases of broader societal phenomena which have occupied different types of social scientists for some time past. Thus, instead of attempting to construct an independent set of concepts for international business, it is natural to build a conceptual framework by adapting and adding to the ideas already developed in various disciplines.

The next step, therefore, is to analyze the two basic processes of international business according to the applicable concepts from the social sciences. As a practical matter it appears more manageable to pursue a three-pronged approach dealing with the two processes separately in what may be called their constructive or positive aspects and then adding as the third prong certain conflict elements which are relevant to both of the processes.

1 The positive side of the *transmission of resources* proceeds from the essential condition for virtually all such exchanges that there be mutual benefit with each party gaining by the process of giving up some resources in return for others. The issues in this context lie in determining which resources may be effectively and profitably transmitted and what means of transmission should be employed. The initial approach to the conceptual framework here is found in international economic theory, but it must be modified to fit the political-economic patterns found in the real world, and the characteristics of the multinational firm.

International economic theory is not entirely adequate for this conceptual analysis because it is largely directed toward trade flows, and there is no theory which encompasses transmission of all types of resources. However, it seems reasonable and of practical utility to apply the basic ideas contained in existing theory, notably comparative advantage and resource allocation, to develop a concept of economic differentials among nations as fundamental forces affecting the flow of resources. The concept is then modified by recognition of the governmental influences which either distort the differentials or directly intervene in the transmission process so that the resources flow in a different manner than they would if governed only by free-market forces.

The analysis to this point provides a basis for determining the opportunities for resource transmission available to the multinational firm. The opportunities it accepts are then determined by its corporate characteristics which generally include concern with market penetration, long-term profit maximization, and financial conservatism. Thus, while there are typically major opportunities for transmission of both capital and skills, the multinational firm is generally found to concentrate on the latter, employing the former more as a useful aid to control the effective transmission of skills than as a primary objective. The conceptual scheme along these lines also deals effectively with the basic policy questions as to the method of transmission employed, for example, the choice between licensing and controlled subsidiaries. In view of the primary emphasis on skill transmission, licensing appears a direct and simple transmission method; but the general preference for subsidiaries in terms of this analysis fits better with the corporate desire for long-term market penetration.

2   The positive side of *relations with host societies* is concerned essentially with the determination of a pattern of operations for the multinational firm which will result in the most profitable accommodation with the local national environment. The fundamental issues in this process lie in choices between conformity and innovation. Inevitably the business systems of the parent multinational firm will differ in some and often many and significant ways from those common to the host society. Thus the process of operating across a national border repeatedly involves determinations as to whether to conform to the host business system or to attempt to inject some degree of change into the prevailing pattern. To grapple with these questions, we may draw from the behavioral sciences concepts which explain what makes business systems function and lead toward a workable conceptual approach to determining when and how innovation may be introduced in them.

Fundamental to the analysis here are two concepts: first, that each society has an internally consistent and complete system of economic and interpersonal relationships and, second, that the dominant patterns of these relationships are subject to change over time as new patterns prove to be functionally more effective for the society. The key factor in relating the multinational firm to these concepts is its role as a foreign transmitter of resources, notably of new skills. Although the first concept provides a general logic for conforming to the prevailing system of relationships in the society, the concept of change in the direction of more effective patterns fits best with the role of the multinational firm. Thus we are led to a concept of strategy in which efforts to achieve change are the primary objective to be guided by determinations as to whether the changes will be functional within the society. Conformity is then the residual strategy pursued where change appears to be dysfunctional.

3 Although the international business processes must necessarily be positive or constructive on balance to justify their existence, they almost invariably include elements of conflict, often strong ones. The conflicts stem from the efforts motivated by both logic and emotion of parties on either side of national borders to protect and advance their relative positions. The issues for management lie in determining what its objectives and positions should be in handling conflict situations. Since much of the conceptual framework relevant to the conflicts is pertinent to both transmission of resources and relations with host societies, it is most efficient to treat it separately rather than duplicating the discussion in the analysis of both types of processes (number 3 in Figure 1.2).

The conflicts can be defined as largely falling within the areas of *nationalism and national interest,* for which concepts developed in political science and economics are useful. The emotional content of nationalism centers on the internal cohesion of the national "we-group" and its resistance to outsiders. Since by definition the multinational firm seeks to penetrate the territory of the we-group at least to some degree for purposes of control of operations and profit, there is an inherent conflict between it and the host nationalism. This conflict adds an emotional component to the practical issues of national interest involved in the resource transmission process and the interactions with the host society. In this process, the multinational firm serves in a sense as the agent for the national interests of its parent country; so there is a confrontation of national interests.

The resolution of these conflicts has two phases: the reduction of the range of conflict by definition of interests and the negotiation of the residual conflict upon the basis of power relationships. The analysis of the first phase is concerned both with minimization of the effect of nationalism which tends to becloud the views of both sides as to what their true national interests are as well as the specific logics of the interests involved in each issue. Although it is possible to reduce the range of conflict to some extent in this manner, it is assumed that there will usually be some residual difference between the positions of the host nation and the multinational firm. The resolution of the conflict will then, it is postulated, turn on the strength of the economic and political power which each party can command. In this relative-power concept, change over time is noted as an important variable, with the tendency in recent years for the power of host countries to rise relative to that of the multinational firms.

The conceptual framework to this point then has three facets: a politico-economic approach to transmission of resources modified by certain concepts of the nature of corporations, a social science approach to patterns of business relations with host societies, and a politico-economic approach to conflicts with nationalism and national interest applicable in part to both transmission of resources and relations with host societies. This framework appears to be adequate to encompass the international business processes found in operations involving a parent multinational firm and one foreign country.

It is not sufficient, though, to encompass the issues arising for the multinational firm from the fact that it operates in more than one and usually many countries. Although the basic disciplines provide ideas relevant to the multicountry operations, they have not as yet developed concepts which are particularly helpful in their resolution. The conceptual framework at this point therefore strikes out independently and in a much less sophisticated form.

The conflict between *fragmentation* and *unification* is the concept which appears to be most useful in dealing with the multicountry operation issues. The main elements of this issue are summarized in Figure 1.3. The underlying theme throughout the single-country analysis was the development of a pattern of policies and practices best suited for each country. Because of the diversity of environments, such an approach leads inevitably toward a diversified or fragmented global pattern. The multicountry orientation, however, introduces counterforces arguing for a unified pattern. The advantages of being a global firm, summarized on the left in Figure 1.3 including the parent-company capabilities and the global-system potentials, can best be realized when there is a

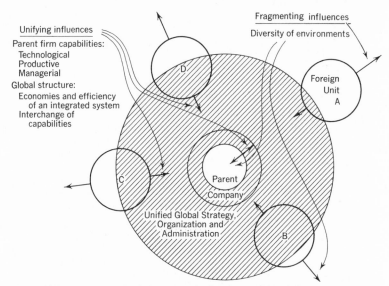

Figure 1.3 A conceptual framework for international business: multi-nation relationships.

substantial amount of unification in the operations. The fragmentation-unification conflict is significant in a number of issues including product policy, logistic plans, and ownership.

As Figure 1.3 suggests, one finds in the typical multinational system some aspects of the operations of each unit (including the parent firm) which fall outside the range of unification, the degree of departure varying from country to country. In this case, for example, A may be a licensee in Japan whose activities are quite different from those of the multinational firm except for some shared technology. B could be a fully owned subsidiary in Canada, where the similarity of conditions has permitted operations to take essentially the same form as those of the U.S. parent firm. The varying strength of the unifying and fragmenting forces from country to country and from company to company precludes any generally applicable pattern. Their resolution lies, therefore, in balancing the benefits in each case. Although the conceptual development is inadequate yet to provide very clear guidelines for the proper balance, it is here proposed that the main thrust in the balance should be toward the unification side. Since the unique characteristic of the multinational firm as distinguished from national firms is its global character, its strength, and presumably therefore its special contributions to society and its survival, should come from the realization of the unification capabilities.

The basic components of the conceptual framework have now been laid out. The interconnected processes of transmission of resources and relations with host societies are the distinctive aspects of an international business as distinguished from a domestic one. These processes are considered in two ways: first, as mutually beneficial, constructive activities for both the multinational firm and the interests of the affected nations and, second, as they involve elements of conflict related to the confrontation of the interests of the firm with different national interests and nationalistic attitudes. Analysis along these lines with respect to operations in individual foreign countries leads toward a fragmented, diversified pattern of policies and activities. The fragmentation, however, weakens the effectiveness of the multinational corporation whose unique potentials vis-à-vis local national firms lie largely in its unified, global capabilities. The achievement of balance between fragmentation and unification therefore composes the final element in the conceptual framework.

These elements provide the overall conceptual framework for the full range of uniquely *international* aspects of the multinational firm. For the presentation of the framework in this book, a further subdivision of the subject has been found useful—namely, treatment of business policies and practices as one entity and of organization and administration as another. Since the underlying concepts are the same for both, it should theoretically be possible to combine them; and at some later date, perhaps such a treatment will be written. For the time being, however, it seems to be much more manageable to separate the two. Thus the next four chapters deal with the main conceptual components as applied to policies and practices: Chapter 2 on transmission of resources, Chapter 3 on relations with host societies, Chapter 4 on conflicts with nationalism and national interests, and Chapter 5 on global strategies involving the fragmentation-unification issue. Then in Chapter 6 all these conceptual components are blended in a composite treatment of organization and administration.

One limitation in the analysis presented in the book must be noted. The discussion focuses specifically on companies engaged in manufacturing and related marketing activities. The basic concepts advanced would seem pertinent to other types of international business—extractive operations, banks, advertising agencies, and so forth. However, the application of the concepts in each type of business has different features. For practical purposes, therefore, it has proved more workable to proceed through the application process with respect only to the multinational industrial firm. The word "industrial" will usually be omitted for the sake of brevity, but it is implied wherever the term *multinational firm* or *corporation* is used.

Since one can find assorted definitions of the term *multinational firm* in the literature, a few words about it are also required. The usage here is concerned solely with structural characteristics. It is applied to all firms which engage directly in business activities in two or more countries. Other definitions go further. For example, some define multinational firms as those with stockholders in more than one country or those with a worldwide managerial outlook. But, for the purpose of this book, the only criterion is that the firm be directly involved in international operations such as exporting, licensing, and operation of controlled factories abroad.

SUGGESTED SUPPLEMENTAL READINGS

Before launching into the development of this conceptual framework, the assumptions which have been made about the reader should be stated. Probably the book will be informative to a person with no prior knowledge of international business. But full comprehension of its content will call for a background of fundamentals which have not been set forth in this short volume. For those readers who do not have this background, initial reading of a few other books is recommended: for the environment of international business—Roy Blough, *International Business* (McGraw-Hill Book Company, New York, 1966); for the functional aspects of international operations—John Fayerweather, *Management of International Operations* (McGraw-Hill Book Company, New York, 1960); and for the public-policy issues (taxation, balance of payments, etc.)—John Fayerweather, *Facts and Fallacies of In-*

ternational Business (Holt, Rinehart and Winston, Inc., New York, 1962). In addition, it would be helpful to have a grasp of the basic concepts of international economics which are available in numerous texts of which the following may be cited: Seymour E. Harris, *International and Interregional Economics* (McGraw-Hill Book Company, New York, 1957); Charles P. Kindleberger, *International Economics* (Richard D. Irwin, Inc., Homewood, Ill., 1963); and Peter F. Kenen, *International Economics* (Prentice-Hall, Inc., Englewood Cliffs, N.J., 1967). There are a number of other books and articles which may be fruitfully read for further background. With the content of the suggested books well in hand, however, the reader will have an adequate background to think through the ideas which are advanced in the chapters to follow. For the reader who wishes to explore certain aspects of this subject to a greater depth, there is a list of supplementary readings at the end of the book.

Chapter Two
International Transmission of Resources

A sound starting point for the construction of a conceptual framework for the multinational firm is its role in the economic relations among nations. Essentially that role is to transmit resources between countries in response to opportunities created by the unequal distribution of resource supply-demand patterns. In this chapter we will look at the three major factors which bear on the performance of this role: the basic economic differentials, the influence of governments on the process of resource transmission, and the relevant characteristics of the multinational corporation. The combined effect of these factors will then be considered as they bear on the types of resources which companies attempt to transmit and the manner in which they accomplish the transmission.

In this discussion resources are considered as falling into six categories: natural resources, capital, labor, and technological, managerial, and entrepreneurial skills. This grossly oversimplifies the situation because in any one resource category, there will be many components, each with its own intercountry differentials. A breakdown of technological skills, for example, could be carried through many levels to such refinements as that between ability to synthesize two distinct chemical products. However, recognizing that for each firm the analysis would have to be pursued in much greater ramification, we can develop the main strategic considerations from these six categories.

Resources may also be transmitted in various forms. The transmission can be in segregated form, for example, capital moving through the purchase of securities of foreign companies with no accompanying management participation (i.e., portfolio investment). But most of the transmission process involves combinations of resources. Exports of goods typically represent varying portions of natural resources, capital (in the form of depreciation of the machinery used to make them), labor, and skills. A capital investment resulting in establishment of a factory abroad is usually accompanied by commitments of technological, managerial, and entrepreneurial skills carried in part by management personnel (a form of labor resources). The conceptual framework must, therefore, take account of a great variety of mixes in the resource transmission process of international business.

At the outset we should distinguish the resource transmission role of the multinational firm from that of the strictly national firm. Regional differentials in resources can, of course, be found within any single country, at least to some degree, and in the larger countries like the United States, to a substantial degree. The key distinction in the international sphere lies in the identification of resource differentials with individual countries. For example, although there are differences between regions of the United States in the availability of capital or the level of skills of workers, there is an overall national level of these resources which is notably different from the level in, say, India. Furthermore, the differentials among nations have been notably influenced by institutional restrictions constructed on a national basis which directly affect the conduct of international business. Differentials in skills, for example, are affected by immigration restrictions which have limited the movement of peoples. Thus, as compared to the strictly national enterprise, the multinational firm is concerned, first, with the resource differentials among nations and, second, with the national institutional restraints which affect the flow of these resources among nations.

BASIC ECONOMIC RELATIONSHIPS

Economic theory provides the foundation for constructing concepts concerning the transmission of resources. Economists have for many years been occupied with relations between nations. Although there are still gaps in their theories, they have laid out an approach which is basically adequate for our purposes here. Essentially they have focused on formulating concepts which account for the economic transactions between nations in terms of the differentials among them.

The main body of theory in this field deals with trade which historically has been more prominent than investments, licensing, and other types of international business activity. The origins of modern trade theory lie in Adam Smith's concepts of international specialization developed in the eighteenth century. A key element was added in 1817 by David Ricardo in his theory of comparative advantage to which two Swedes, Bertil Ohlin and Eli Heckscher, contributed a vital component based on the distribution of resources in 1933. The comparative-advantage, resource-distribution approach has persisted to this day as the basic doctrine of the field with the more recent efforts of economists primarily concerned with attempts to apply and to test its concepts.

The main proposition in the basic theory is that nations export those products which they can produce most efficiently and import those in which they are least efficient as compared with other nations. In establishing the relationships, we noted that the dominant differentials are usually found in the availability of various resources used in production. Differentials in other cost factors such as transportation and size of production units also play a part as do differences in demand patterns.

Although substantial absolute differentials in resource distribution can be observed, these differentials are not controlling because of the necessity for balance in transactions among countries. To cite an extreme case to point up the limitations, one country might in absolute terms have a supply of all categories of resources superior to another country. Clearly, there would not be a net outflow of all categories of products from it, for this would result in its giving away its wealth for no compensation. The comparative-advantage approach therefore postulates that a country will export those products which it is relatively best equipped to produce and import those in which it is least efficient. With appropriate adjustments of the foreign-exchange rate between countries, the prices of the products a country makes most efficiently will be competitive in world markets, and those in which it is least efficient will be noncompetitive. Thus, for example, the cost of a particular German-made machine tool might be 20,000 marks and that of a fine rug made in Germany 10,000 marks. The same items if made in Turkey might cost 100,000 lira and 10,000 lira, respectively. With the exchange rate of 3 lira per mark, Germany would sell the machine tools to Turkey and import rugs from Turkey.

The Ohlin-Heckscher approach identifies the unequal distribution of resources which affects costs of production as the main determinant of the comparative-advantage differentials. Thus the ratio of the supply of capital to labor in Germany is relatively much greater than in Turkey. Since machine-tool production requires greater portions of capital than making rugs, the Germans are comparatively more efficient in making the machine tools than rugs as indicated by the fact that the price of the German-made machine tool is twice that of the German-made rug, whereas for Turkish-made products the ratio is 10 to 1. Beyond the dominant-resource differentials, the analysis would have to consider any other factors which might affect the costs. For example, German machine-tool makers may benefit from larger-scale output through access to the large European market, compared with the smaller local market a Turkish maker could serve. The latter would, however, have a transportation cost advantage in his home market.

Finally, demand differentials must also be incorporated into the theory. In country 1 resource X may be very scarce, but because there is negligible demand, it commands a lower price than resource Y which is more plentiful but in strong demand. In country 2 the demand for both resources might be strong. If the distribution of resources in country 2 were the same as in country 1, the greater demand for resource X would result in a relatively higher price for it than in country 1. Thus country 2 would tend to import products incorporating resource X. The influence of this sort of difference in demand patterns is probably most significant in the flow of raw materials required in industrial products. Many raw materials are available in less developed countries whose industries have only modest needs for them. In the absence of external demand, their prices might be quite low. The relatively greater demand in the industrially advanced countries results in higher world prices, however, and substantial export flows. Thus, although resource-distribution differentials are generally the stronger factor, demand differentials do play a part in the economics of raw-material trade. For finished consumer products the demand-differential influences do not generally have as great an effect on prices, but to some degree they are doubtless always present.

To summarize, the theory proposes that the structure of trade flows will be determined by what may be called the effective differentials in the distribution of resources among countries. The stronger influence is assumed to come from differentials in proportions of resources available within countries. The qualification "effective" recognizes the modifying influence on these patterns of differences in other cost factors and in the demand structures of countries.[1]

The basic trade theory evolved at a time when economic data were very sparse. With the great increase in available statistics and techniques for utilizing them, economists in recent years have made intensive efforts to apply and test the theory on real trade relations. Some tests have supported the theory and some have seemed to discredit it, notably a study of U.S. trade conducted by Wassily Leontief which showed that U.S. exports were labor-intensive rather than capital-intensive as should be true if the theory were valid.[2] However, it seems quite likely that the problem lies not so much with the theory as with the difficulty of applying it. Two recent studies have shown that comparative advantage in research and development leads to strong exports of high technology products.[3] Another study suggests that skill in product innovation, which includes not only technology but managerial and entrepreneurial resources, is a basis for exports.[4] Inclusion of data on these skill resources is a substantial advance over the limited

[1] The reader who wishes to go beyond this very brief description of the basis of international intercourse should consult textbooks on international economics like those listed in Chap. 1.

[2] W. S. Leontief, "Domestic Production and Foreign Trade: The American Capital Position Re-examined," *Economia Internazionale,* 1954, or *American Economic Review,* November, 1956, pp. 386–407.

[3] Donald B. Keesing, "The Impact of Research and Development on United States Trade," *Journal of Political Economy,* February, 1967, pp. 38–48; and W. Gruber, D. Mehta, and R. Vernon, "The R & D Factor in International Trade and International Investment of United States Industries," *Journal of Political Economy,* February, 1967, pp. 20–37.

[4] Raymond Vernon, "International Investment and International Trade in the Product Cycle," *The Quarterly Journal of Economics,* May, 1966, pp. 190–207.

labor-capital analysis of Leontief, but economists still have quite a way to go before they are able to inject good statistical data on all types of resources for many countries in the theoretical trade model and thus to clearly prove or disprove it. In the meantime, the basic soundness of the theory which has stood for some years appears to be supported by logic, by general observation of the composition of trade, and by the overall impressions of various tests from trade data. Thus, even though it is not clearly proved, the trade theory is accepted here as sufficiently established to serve as a basis for our conceptual framework.

Theory incorporating all forms of resource transmission, not just the trade component, is notable by its absence from economic literature. Economists recognize the movement of resources (factors of production) and discuss some aspects of the process. For example, the international transfer of capital has been studied extensively. Differences in interest rates which are indicators of effective differentials in capital resource supply-demand relations and marginal productivity in different countries are cited as primary forces governing the flow of capital. But there is no comprehensive scheme which relates the flows of natural resources, capital, labor, and various skills. One problem lies in the fact that some flows, notably the independent emigration of people, involve little or no monetary transfer. But this is not an element in the work of multinational firms, so it would suffice to have a theory covering only exchanges of resources appearing in balance-of-payments data.

Even this will be slow in evolving because of the difficulty of sorting out and especially of quantifying the components. For example, licensing agreements result in transfer of technological skills in exchange for, let us say, raw materials (with intervening monetary transactions). But the supply of the skills in the licensing company is not reduced by the transfer, so it is difficult for the economist to develop an effective price theory for licensing which would be essential to a theory based on price relationships. Likewise, how is one to determine the relative availability of entrepreneurial resources in various countries? This is a fascinating question which has occupied many people concerned with economic development. As yet, however, differences have only been identified to a very crude degree by qualitative methods, typically by sociological approaches, rather than by economists using quantifiable measures.

Despite this lack of economic theory, there would seem to be logic in extending to the whole resource transmission process the philosophy embodied in the trade theory. Both in it and in such theory as there is concerning direct resource movements, the influence of effective differentials in resource distribution is consistent with a comprehensive theory of resource transmission. Thus in this chapter it is assumed as a general proposition that basic economic forces work toward outflows from each country of those resources which it has in relatively most plentiful supply—"relative" being a function of demand and the supply-demand structure for other resources both in the country and in other countries.

This proposition may be illustrated in the economic relations of the two countries shown schematically in Figure 2.1. The bars on either side indicate the level of availability of resources in the countries. It is presumed that country B, being in most categories notably poorer than country A, will export natural resources and labor, even though its supply of the former is less and of the latter much the same as that of country A in absolute terms. No demand differentials have been indicated in the figure. If country A is an industrialized nation and country B one of the underdeveloped nations, the demand for natural resources and labor is likely to be lower in B than in A because of underdeveloped industry and unemployment. These demand differences would give further impetus to the directions of the resource flows shown in the figure.

The form in which a given resource is transmitted—either directly (i.e., in separate or pure form) or indirectly in combination with other resources—is a function of its own characteristics and of the differentials in distribution of other resources. Some resources cannot be moved—land and water power for example—so the values they produce can only be transmitted indirectly through the movement of other resource forms. Thus aluminum raw material is transported several thousand miles from the Caribbean to Kitimat in western Canada to utilize the plentiful water power available there, and the refined aluminum is reshipped to various world markets. Other resources can be moved with varying degrees of difficulty. Labor can be transferred from country to country as amply demonstrated by the employment, in the 1960s, of some 2.5 million temporary workers in Germany, Switzerland, and other European countries, imported from Italy,

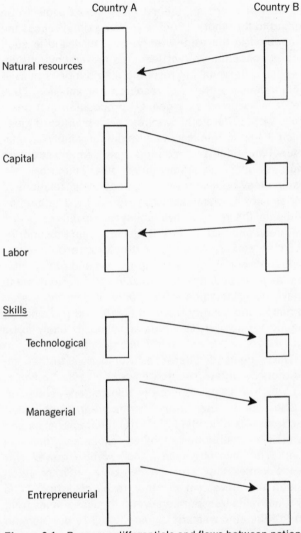

Figure 2.1 Resource differentials and flows between nations.

Spain, Greece, and as far away as Turkey. But such movements are relatively awkward, especially for long distances and where language and other differences complicate the utilization of immigrant workers. It is very common, therefore, to find labor resources transmitted in combination with other resources in manufactured goods.

Capital can quite readily be transmitted directly. But it is often more efficiently utilized if it is invested in the supplying country in industrial plants and the products made in the plants shipped instead. The critical consideration is generally the size of the production facilities and the resultant economies of scale. The manufacture of heavy industrial equipment sold in quite small volume in many markets is a prime example. It would be possible to export capital to set up small factories in each country. But the low volume of each plant would result in much higher costs than would be achieved in a single large plant in one country. Thus the capital resource transmission is accomplished more efficiently in this case indirectly in the form of exports of finished equipment which embody the services of capital combined with natural resource, labor, and skill components.

The economic differentials of each of the various resources affect the types of combinations which are suitable for the transmission process. The more economical combination is the one in which the content is predominantly drawn from resources in which the transmitting country has a relative advantage, and the less economical is the one in which a large portion of resources in which it does not have an advantage are incorporated. Two examples from U.S. commerce serve as illustrations. Certain chemical products prosper as exports because they use natural gas which is plentiful and are made in highly automated plants requiring large capital investments and a few very skilled workers. On the other hand, U.S. automobile exports show a long-term decline because, despite substantial capital and skill components, they incorporate also considerable labor and raw-material content in both of which the United States is relatively deficient. Thus it has increasingly proved more economical to transmit such capital and skills as were needed abroad and manufacture there, especially as foreign markets have grown.

At the present state of economic skills, it is difficult to quantify individual components of this picture and impossible to develop any meaningful overall mathematical model which would determine their relationship. However, in general terms, the flows found in international business confirm the validity of the economic forces postulated by the concept. The pattern of U.S. foreign transactions which conforms roughly to that shown in Figure 2.1 is a good illustration. In four of the categories the United States is visibly better off than virtually all countries. Using differences in interest rates as a rough criterion, we can safely conclude that its capital resources are relatively more plentiful than those in virtually all other countries. Thus there is a net outflow of capital. Differentials in technological skills are quite readily observed in the performance superiority of a wide range of U.S. products in less developed countries and even on balance in comparison with those of other developed countries. The relative adequacy of managerial skills is not quite so definable; but it is quite commonly accepted as a fact, and the outflow is visible in such forms as the steady expansion of U.S. consulting services abroad and the adoption of U.S. business school methods in foreign countries. The existence of superior entrepreneurial resources can scarcely be demonstrated by any useful measurement, and it may well not be valid in comparisons with many countries. On balance it seems likely that it is valid, however, in light of the apparent net outflow of entrepreneurial talent in U.S. economic relations with the rest of the world.

The compensating inflows into the United States have been dominated by natural resources and labor. The former include petroleum, many minerals, tropical agricultural products, and the like, which are both plentiful and more economically produced in other lands. The labor inflow appears primarily in the predominance in U.S. imports of manufactured goods with a high labor content—textiles, watches, and the like. This category is the best example in the overall U.S. pattern of the *relative* abundance aspect of the differentials. The absolute superiority of the resources of workers in one country versus another is hard to determine and not in any case pertinent. The only meaningful comparison is the relation between the labor supply and the capacity of a country to use it productively. The United States, by virtue of its advanced industrial development, is able to employ workers more productively than other countries; and therefore it is short of labor, relative both to its own supply of other resources and the labor supply abroad.

GOVERNMENTAL INFLUENCES

Although the overall pattern of international transmission of resources is governed by the basic economic relationships in their
distribution in and among nations, there are many distortions in
the pattern induced by government actions. In the pursuit of various national objectives, governments may alter the effective relationships or directly intervene in the flow of resources.

Altering the effective relationships is accomplished by any measure which changes the price of a resource relative to the price of
another resource. In our modern, monetized societies all the economic relationships we have been discussing are stated in terms of
prices—wages, interest rates, prices of commodities, and so forth.
The prices stated in terms of national currencies are related inter-
nationally by means of exchange rates. The prices of each resource and the exchange rates in the straightforward economic
scheme outlined above will have shifted in response to supply-and-
demand relationships to reach a level at which the appropriate
flows will take place. If a government action alters a price therefore, the amount or direction of flows will tend to change away from
the pattern that had prevailed under the pure economic forces.

The government actions pertinent to this discussion affect two
types of price relationships: the overall differences between nations and those between nations for individual resources. In the
first category fall internal fiscal, monetary, and other policies
which affect the general price level and regulation of exchange
rates which affect the overall translation of internal prices into
currencies of other nations. The result of a change in either the
overall price level or the exchange rate of a nation is to cause a
general shift in the apparent relative level of all of its resources.
For example, if government policies cause a general inflation, the
prices of each resource rise just as they would individually if their
supply were actually limited. The international effect therefore is
to attract greater flows of these resources from other nations, or if
the prevailing flow has been outward for a particular resource, the
effect is to reduce the outflow. An alteration in the exchange rate
has essentially the same effect—changing the apparent across-the-

board relationship of national prices and either attracting or discouraging resource flows. For the country whose overall price level is raised, the result is not only an increase in the tendency of individual resources to flow toward it but also a tendency toward a shift in the net balance of resource flows. If as a consequence the total inflows and outflows are unequal, some further change must come to restore the balance either in the internal price level or exchange rates or in one or more of the ways to be discussed below.

International price relationships of individual resources may be altered by governments in a number of ways, chiefly by various forms of taxation and subsidies. The most common form of taxation employed is the tariff whose effect is to raise the price of foreign goods relative to internal prices and thus to discourage them from flowing into the country. Though less common, taxes can be applied to affect international flows of other types of resources. For example, in 1964, the United States imposed an interest equalization tax on issues of foreign securities in the United States which in effect raised the interest rates (prices of capital) and thus discouraged the outflow of U.S. capital.

Subsidies typically are employed with the opposite effect. The government of a country makes some financial contribution to the supplier of a resource which permits the latter to sell at lower prices and encourages outflow of the resource from the country. The common form is the use of export subsidies which reduce the prices of certain products relative to those of other countries.

Direct *intervention in the flow of resources* can be accomplished by a government through the exercise of various controls over movements across its borders. Such regulations are commonly found restricting many types of flows: quotas restraining importing of products, exchange controls limiting the flow of capital, emigration and immigration restrictions regulating the movement of people, national security rules forbidding the transmission of certain technological skills, and so forth.

From the point of view of the policies of the multinational firm, we are concerned not only with the ways in which governments may influence the flows of resources but also with understanding the reasons for their actions as a basis for predicting government policies and relating company policies to them. Looking at the range of government actions during the era since World War II, we can discern three main patterns: efforts to foster economic development, moves to protect national groups, and measures to deal with balance-of-payments deficits.

The concept of government initiative and control to further *economic development* is firmly established in the less developed countries and even to varying degrees in the advanced countries. To the extent that international flows of resources are important to economic development, it is common to find governments using their influence toward this end. Although there are assorted philosophies as to how to further economic development, a few guidelines are widely accepted and thus recur frequently in patterns of government action. The main emphasis typically is upon development of national industrial production, so efforts are made to encourage the inflow of resources which contribute to this goal—especially capital, skills, and essential natural resources—and to discourage the inflow of finished products in which local production is being fostered. A second and related guideline is the desire to concentrate the utilization of receipts from the outflow of resources on uses which contribute to industrial development. This leads to controls which restrict the inflow of resources which are not regarded as essential, notably those incorporated in luxury goods. Third, efforts are made to decrease dependence upon foreign resources, an objective contributing to national security, economic strength, and nationalistic pride. This objective can lead to restriction of flows of any resource, ranging from limitations on employment of expatriate technicians which force the training of local nationals to "buy national" regulations requiring that locally made products be favored in government procurement.

Protection of national groups often runs counter to the best interests of a country in maximizing economic growth, but it is a common feature of society nonetheless. Individuals and groups with established economic activities seek to protect their positions. They may be able to obtain government support from internal threats, but they are likely to be most successful if the threat is from foreigners because of their superior political status as compared with outsiders, a subject to be discussed in Chapter 4. Thus it is quite common to find obstacles to the inflow of resources constructed to protect established economic interests. The commonest form of protection is the tariff which raises the prices of imported goods. Less commonly, the same end is achieved by import quotas or direct subsidies to local industries. Restrictions of this nature may be applied to other resource flows. For example, when small retailers in Mexico were threatened by the modern merchandising and entrepreneurial skills of Sears, Roebuck, they sought (though unsuccessfully) to have the government forbid foreign companies to enter the retailing field.

Measures taken to deal with *balance-of-payments deficits* vary greatly both in type and in the sophistication of government actions bearing on them. There have been cases, like Italy's imposition of modest measures to reduce imports in 1963, where minor interference with economic relationships, soundly managed, were evidently effective in solving a transitory problem without serious distortion of resource transmission patterns. There have been others, of which the United States is the notable case, where measures of increasing magnitude affecting particularly capital flows have substantially distorted natural economic relationships, though it is not at all clear what those relationships should be. Because of the overriding concern for maintaining the strength of the U.S. dollar as an international reserve currency, most responsible authorities have felt that controls could not be released and natural economic relationships are not, therefore, allowed to assert themselves.

Finally there have been a host of examples, chiefly among the less developed countries, of governments which have encountered balance-of-payments problems which have been caused by and perpetuated by various national shortcomings. In the typical case, the country is relatively immature politically, so that its government is unstable and its bureaucracy not very competent. These conditions result in the government pursuing unwise economic policies both from lack of competence and from fear of taking actions which may have adverse political impact. From these conditions emerge government deficits, wasteful use of government funds, and inflation. The inflation distorts the overall level of resource prices in relation to the rest of the world. The apparently sound economic corrective should be a change of the country's exchange rate to reverse the distortion. At this point, however, inertia and national pride act to deter a devaluation, which is generally viewed as harmful to national prestige. So the country solves the imbalance in the economic pressures by other means, chiefly restrictions permitting entry only of favored classifications of resources. The net effect of all of this is to limit the natural flow of some resources while others receive an unnatural push because of the price distortions.

CORPORATE CHARACTERISTICS

The economic differentials and government actions establish the range of opportunities and limitations within which corporate strategies may be formulated. The selection of actual strategies is dependent upon factors within the corporation itself. The multinational corporation is not in its nature given to opportunistic, short-term profit maximization. It does not, therefore, exploit fully all economic differentials between nations, nor does it function with full flexibility in those which it does exploit. In the total international business community, there are individuals and groups that are both more opportunistic and more flexible—consultants, individual investors, traders, and the like. These tend to accomplish much of the flow of resources and as such serve a vital economic function. The multinational corporation is limited, therefore, to the role for which its characteristics are suitable.

The crucial characteristics of the corporation are that it has a finite combination of resources under ready control and that it has certain basic policies which govern the directions in which it moves. The critical resources are managerial and technical manpower and capital. Management of overseas operations requires individuals who are technically competent, familiar with a company's methods, and able to command the trust of senior executives. The number of parent country and local nationals meeting these criteria available to a given company at a particular time is always limited. A few companies have tried to expand their international operations rapidly by recruiting personnel without rigorous attention to the essential criteria. However, their results have not been notably successful and for most companies availability of manpower is a key constraint.

Availability of financial resources is a limiting factor chiefly for medium- and small-sized companies. Large companies typically have sufficient capital either within their own resources or through ready access to capital markets so that they can finance any undertaking they feel is sound. In a few cases, the accumulation of financial resources is known to have been a factor encouraging over-seas activities. For the most part, however, it appears that in the larger companies, the supply of financial resources is a neutral factor in determining strategic plans. Among smaller companies, the financial limitations are often a factor restraining their capabilities.

The management policies which affect international strategic planning tend to cluster around quite restricted patterns. The chief objective of the typical corporation is to make its business grow and make profits over the long term by expanding its market position. In the accomplishment of this goal, it has been conditioned to acceptance of considerable risk in technological and marketing innovation. On the whole, however, managements demonstrate substantial conservatism and particularly so with respect to finance. Their approach to the employment of capital resources is generally one of minimizing risk rather than seeking maximum potential return. Within this general pattern there are, of course, many minor variations and not a few major ones.

In pursuit of their objectives, most corporations have also found that they perform most effectively in certain patterns with respect to the structure of operations and grouping of people. A typical concern, for example, engages in some applied research but relies on other institutions for basic research; it does a substantial amount of manufacturing but also purchases many components from other firms; it conducts much of its own marketing operations but delegates a large portion of its advertising design to an agency and so on through the range of business activities. The pattern for each company is partly the result of the logics of the situation in which it operates—its product, market, etc.—and partly a matter of individual style, there being firms in the same industry which operate in different patterns. But regardless of the origins of the pattern, the corporation has become accustomed to its mode of operation, and a substantial part of its effectiveness is attributable to its ongoing competence in functioning in this pattern.

DEVELOPMENT OF CORPORATE STRATEGY

Within the limits set by economic differentials, government actions, and corporation characteristics, the scope for management discretion in transmission of resources is not great. To a large degree it is concerned with deciding whether or not to exploit opportunities and keeping up with changes in the economic and governmental aspects of the situation. At any given moment the directions in which it can effectively move are limited by the potentials of the structure and pattern of operations which provide the basis for the strength it has achieved to that point. In the development of its international operations it has a natural inclination to extend the basic pattern of its domestic activities, though over time it tends to adopt variations in that pattern which prove more appropriate to the international environment. The general pattern of evolution of strategies of companies along these lines will be reviewed below, and then key aspects of the strategy decisions analyzed to extend the conceptual framework.

The manner in which corporate resources and policies affect the resource transmission process can be seen in the typical evolution of the international business of a U.S. manufacturing firm.[5] The first international effort is usually the export of products which is undertaken essentially as a simple expansion of established domestically oriented marketing. The exported products represent a combination of resources which compose an economical form of transmission. For U.S. companies this frequently means the dom-

[5] The discussion in this section does not include the effect of the personal attitudes of individual executives, which studies of international business decisions invariably show are often controlling in the evolution of international operations. Whether or not a firm responds positively to an investment opportunity frequently depends upon whether one or two high-ranking men have a real interest in international operations, and the form and location of investments may be attributable to their particular interests or points of view. Thus to some degree the response of corporations is a personal-social process, rather than a rational-economic one. Although this characteristic is recognized, no attempt has been made to incorporate it into the conceptual framework at this point because we are concerned here with the substantive elements relevant to decision making, not the decision-making process itself. Some of the personal-social aspects which are especially relevant to international business will be considered in Chap. 6; others will not be discussed because they are common to all corporate decision making. Readers interested in discussions of the personal element in international investment decisions should consult: Richard D. Robinson, *International Business Policy,* Holt, Rinehart and Winston, Inc., New York, 1964, pp. 146–218; and Yair Aharoni, *The Foreign Investment Decision Process,* Harvard Business School, Boston, Mass., 1966.

inant content is a superior technology or high capital investment with relatively modest labor and natural resource content. In any case, the combination makes a convenient package of resources acceptable in foreign markets, and so the company establishes itself in international business.

At some point, however, the simple export of products becomes inadequate, and manufacture abroad is undertaken either because the resource differentials change, or because of changes affecting the efficiency of the transmission process, or because of some government action, or because of changes within the corporation. There are many specific possibilities under these headings, but it will suffice here to mention the most common. Important changes in *resource differentials* have occurred because of the increase of the capital and skills available as a result of economic progress in many countries, especially in the advanced industrial nations. Japan, for example, has made rapid advances in electronic technology since World War II and in some phases of that field it is now on a par with other advanced industrial nations. This change, coupled with adequate capital and ample labor, has shifted it from an importer of many electronic products to an exporter, forcing multinational firms to shift from export to Japan to some arrangement based on local manufacture.

The *efficiency of the transmission process* has been notably influenced by the expansion of the size of markets for many products accompanying rising standards of living. Such expansion has made it possible to utilize capital and skills more efficiently in overseas factories. Japan also serves as a good illustration here. Basic production skills have long been established there as evident in the manufacture of products like cameras and sewing machines. But despite low wages, local production of many products was not economical previously because of the limited demand. Production of sewing machines, for example, commenced in 1923, but up to World War II foreign firms like Singer continued to export into Japan on a large scale.[6] In the postwar era, however, with the tremendous increase in per capita income (about 300 percent from 1953 to 1964) the market for many products has grown so much that mass-production economies are

---

[6] John Fayerweather, *Management of International Operations,* McGraw-Hill Book Company, New York, 1960, pp. 541–546.

feasible and local manufacture is far more economical than impor- tation. Thus Japan has not only ceased the importation of sewing machines, but it has become a powerful exporter in that field, forc- ing Singer to join with a Japanese firm to establish a manufac- turing base to supply local customers and world markets previ- ously served more economically from other sources.

The relevant *government actions* have been largely directed at fostering local manufacture by various incentives and restrictions. Illustrations abound, especially among the less developed coun- tries. As noted earlier, one of the main approaches to economic development is to foster local manufacture of a product by such measures as cutting off imports through direct restrictions or high tariffs. Such measures have led multinational firms to set up facto- ries in many countries even though the economic differentials re- sulted in costs considerably higher than those in plants from which they had been exporting.

The response of a company to these changes depends heavily upon its corporate characteristics both as they exist at a given time and as they evolve over time. The most common pattern in recent years has been along the following lines. First, there is the dom- inant objective of building the long-term strength of the firm which creates strong pressure on management to protect any market which has been established through exports. Every study of inter- national investments in recent years has emphasized in one way or another the crucial importance of market strategy in investment decisions.[7] Second, the essentially conservative philosophy of corporations toward finance and property leads to quite guarded reactions to conditions abroad, especially in those countries where political and economic risks are high. Finally, there is the tendency to meet the new situation by deploying the corporate resources in essentially the same pattern to which the firm is accustomed.

Added together, these factors lead readily to the structure of operations which is most commonly found among multinational

[7] Notably Judd Polk et al., *U.S. Production Abroad and the Balance of Payments,* National Industrial Conference Board, · New York, 1966, pp. 59–61; E. R. Barlow and I. T. Wender, *Foreign Investment and Taxa- tion,* Prentice-Hall, Englewood Cliffs, N.J., 1955, pp. 146–147; and U.S. Department of Commerce, *Factors Limiting United States In- vestment Abroad,* Washington, 1953.

corporations. Manufacturing operations abroad have expanded tremendously, as companies have vigorously sought to build their position in world markets. However, concern over the risks of investment has limited the response in two ways. First, within the limits of their resources (chiefly manpower and, to a lesser degree, capital) managements attempt to concentrate their efforts in the areas with the greatest market potential tempering their decisions by the apparent risks. Figure 2.2 illustrates graphically the significance of this type of strategy with favorable investment decisions tending to fall in the shaded area below the line including some countries which have relatively small markets but also quite low risks, Belgium, for example, and at the other end some quite high-risk countries like Brazil which nonetheless have such large-market potentials that companies are willing to invest in them to assure their long-run market position. There are, of course, investments in other countries but proportionately much fewer than in the low-risk or large-market countries. Within this broad general picture there are notable differences among companies as brought out in Franklin Root's survey of a sample of eighteen U.S. firms.[8] He found that about one-third of the companies made investments chiefly to protect markets which otherwise would be lost because of import restrictions or competition. Companies with such defensive strategies tend to give heavy weight to political risks and thus to avoid investments with substantial risks. On the other hand, about two-thirds of the firms demonstrated an aggressive investment policy oriented toward capitalizing on market opportunities. For them, political risks were viewed less as an obstacle blocking investment than as a condition to be minimized by effective management. For companies in the first category, the line in Figure 2.2 would clearly be lower and further to the right; but for those in the second, it would rise and shift to the left, resulting in a greater percentage of favorable investment decisions.

Second, companies have tended to limit their capital transmission to that necessary to establish the operations and maintain working control over them, drawing on local capital for the balance of their requirements.[9] The desire to maintain control is critical to

[8] Franklin R. Root, "U.S. Business Abroad and the Political Risks," *MSU Business Topics,* Winter, 1968, p. 74.

[9] Judd Polk et al., *op. cit.,* pp. 79, 101.

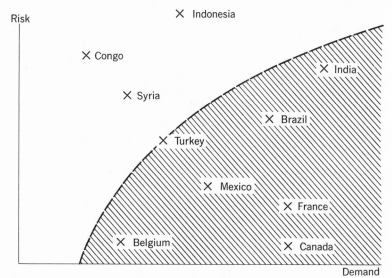

Figure 2.2   Risk, demand, and investment decisions. Shaded area indicates zone of favorable decisions.

the objective of establishing operations abroad which are essentially similar to those at home, permitting the company to function according to its accustomed pattern.

An interesting summary of the response of a company to the various changes in environmental factors is found in a discussion by General Motors' chairman, Frederic Donner, of that firm's major post-World War II strategy decisions.[10] He cites four typical decisions. Two of them—initiation of manufacture in Australia and production of a small car in Europe—were justified by the expansion of markets to the point where local production was feasible. In the Australian case, GM had to import many of the necessary skills; but in the European case, the strong rise of skills among national firms provided a further pressure on General Motors. The third decision cited was the undertaking of production in Argentina despite adverse economic factors because of "our desire to retain a position in a market which . . . appeared to be a reasonable risk from a profit point of view." Because of a combination of government pressures and protection, the company has gone

---

[10] Frederic G. Donner, "The Strategy of a Worldwide Operation," *The McKinsey Quarterly*, Winter, 1967, pp. 36–44.

ahead with production under such conditions in other less developed countries like Brazil and Mexico. The fourth strategic decision discussed by Mr. Donner was the resumption of operations in Germany after World War II despite extensive damage to its factory. A primary factor in this decision was the capacity of the plant to generate sufficient funds for its own reconstruction. GM clearly wanted to have the plant going to serve foreign markets, but the desire to limit the flow of capital from the parent company might well have held the company back if local funds had been insufficient.

In sum, therefore, General Motors' pattern of activities fits the general scheme common to the majority of multinational firms. It initiated international sales by exports, undertaking manufacture abroad when it was forced in that direction by various changes in resource differential patterns or other external factors all the while maintaining full control but with as limited use of U.S. capital as feasible. Overall, there is ample evidence in the growth and profitability of operations which fit this pattern to indicate that it is an effective method of transmitting and utilizing resources abroad. However, it does pose problems which have led in many cases to other patterns and the possibility that further variations may evolve.

Conclusions as to the suitability of each corporate strategy require consideration of which resources a company should attempt to transmit, to what countries they should be transmitted, and what transmission process it should employ, given the combination of economic, government, and corporate factors present. There are a host of variations in the mix among these decisions which we cannot hope to explore. But we can establish the line of analysis required by looking critically at some of the key elements bearing on the three main decision areas.

TYPES OF RESOURCES

The first level of decision as to which resources to transmit is essentially outside the range of management control. That is, the main economic differentials are determined by external economic and government factors and they are, therefore, "givens" in company planning. They establish a particular range of opportunities as feasible and certain others as uneconomic or otherwise impractical. The tasks for management lie, therefore, in identifying the feasible opportunities and deciding which of them it will exploit.

Identifying the feasible opportunities requires a great deal of fact gathering—market studies and the like. But more significantly for our conceptual framework, it is often difficult to perceive in a particular situation whether there is a real resource differential which a firm may in practical terms exploit. Demands for standard commodities can usually be identified quite readily. But as one proceeds through more sophisticated goods and then into the skills, the problem becomes increasingly complex.

The difficulty lies in the distinction between the apparent value of a resource for a country and the actual demand for it. For example, a company might predict that a certain product would be useful to the people of a country, judging by experience in other countries. But if it knows that there is presently resistance for cultural and other reasons to the product, it must determine whether there is a valid resource differential which, with the aid of advertising, can be effectively exploited or whether the differential has no real substance because demand cannot be activated. Likewise, certain human relations practices may be predicted to be quite beneficial for factory supervision in a country, but if there is cultural resistance to them, the validity of the differential will depend upon a judgment as to whether training can overcome the resistance. This problem area clearly projects us into analysis of the character of the countries with which the multinational firm does business, and further consideration of it will therefore be deferred until the next chapter in which the relations between the firm and host societies will be discussed.

Once the feasible opportunities for resource transmission are identified, the multinational firm must decide which it will exploit. Looking at the prevailing activities of multinational industrial firms, we find that they are heavily committed to transmission of skills and relatively less concerned with raw materials, labor, and capital.

The primary attention to skill transmission can be observed most readily in the nature of multinational firms. They are typically skill leaders. Gruber, Mehta, and Vernon have documented this characteristic with respect to technology.[11] They show that not only in

[11] W. Gruber et al., "The R & D Factor in International Trade," *op. cit.,* p. 31.

exports but also in overseas investment research-intensive industries are the leaders. For example, analyzing data on eighteen categories of U.S. manufacturers for 1964, they find that the four with the highest relative research effort had a ratio of investments in Europe compared to those in the United States of 1 to 8, whereas the eighteen less research-oriented firms had a ratio of 1 to 30. Though no comparable data are available for other types of skills, observation of the nature of firms in international business confirms that they are typically the better managed and more aggressive organizations.

The strong commitment to skill transmission can also be seen in another dimension of multinational corporation characteristics. It is generally true of the companies, whether they be skill leaders or followers, that various forms of skill transmission are of first importance in their ongoing operational activities, extending from the supervisory functions of senior executives to the flow of instruction manuals abroad, to the training for foreign personnel in parent-company factories.[12] They add up to a continuing effort to feed assorted skills from the parent organization into the foreign units. The motivation for this activity within the corporation comes from its observation that the application of these skills is competitively advantageous in foreign markets. It finds that by putting various skills to work abroad, it can in one way or another either create new sales or sell better than local competitors or make a larger profit. In terms of our conceptual framework, what this means is that there are skill differentials, and the emphasis on transmitting the skills within the corporation is proving economically effective.

The starting point for this emphasis on skill transmission must, of course, be the existence of substantial skill differentials between countries, but it also has much to do with the nature of the multinational corporation. A large portion of the existing skills useful in industry have been originated or developed for practical application within the firms. This statement does not discount the great contributions of independent scientific laboratories to tech-

---

[12] A good example is provided by the massive dissemination of training programs from the headquarters of International Telephone and Telegraph Corp., transmitting skills to a foreign work force of some 130,000. Ben B. Mason and William Darnow, "Training on a Global Scale: An ITT Speciality," *Worldwide P&I Planning*, March–April, 1968, pp. 38–49.

nology, of consultants and business schools to managerial methods, and of other organizations outside the multinational firms. But as a practical matter a large portion of the skills originating in these groups have been converted to practical utility within the multinational corporations. As a consequence, it is natural that the latter should serve as a primary agent for transmission of skill resources.

There is a good deal of transmission by other means—foreigners attending schools in countries with advanced skills, consultants passing on their know-how to foreign companies, etc.—but the multinational corporation is particularly suited to perform a large part of the task. It has brought skills to an operationally viable stage, and it is structurally equipped to see the transmission process through to operational effectiveness abroad. For example, the skills required for production of a new chemical or marketing a new product are available from several sources. But a manufacturing firm like du Pont or Imperial Chemical Industries is most likely to have brought them all together into an effective package and by a combination of organizational methods including staffing, written manuals, management controls, etc., it is in a position to take them abroad and follow through to assure their effective application. Thus from a societal viewpoint, there is logic in the major emphasis on skill transmission in the multinational firm which gives this emphasis fundamental support in management decision making.

This basic logic finds reinforcement in the competitive characteristics of the corporation. The combination of technology, managerial know-how, and entrepreneurial capability within a firm is typically the source of its greatest strength, and its organizational unity is in itself something unique. That is, the total skill capacity of the firm exceeds the sum of the individual skills of its members because the organization has acquired an ongoing effectiveness. For all its huge size and massive capital a General Electric or an IBM derives the greater part of its strength from its skill resources. This fact is perhaps best demonstrated by the capacity of smaller firms which have an edge in some aspect of technological, managerial, or entrepreneurial capacity to give the giants a sharp competitive fight. Thus in deciding which resources to transmit, it is sound for the multinational firm to give first attention to the skills at its command, for it is clearly well equipped to exploit international skill differentials.

The lesser concern with other forms of resources is due to less favorable mixes of differentials and corporate characteristics. The differentials for natural resources and labor have not generally run in the same direction as the trend of development of the international activities of the companies. There are many exceptions such as products made from natural gas and some agricultural items exported from the United States. But the main evolution of multinational firms has proceeded outward by exports from countries which did not have a comparative advantage in labor and natural resources and toward nations in which they were more readily available. The opportunity which has not been heavily exploited, therefore, is for the most part in the reverse flow of resources back to the parent country. Few multinational industrial firms have aggressively devoted themselves to production in locations where labor and natural resources were plentiful and transmission of these resources in some form to other countries. Most of the activity of this sort has originated with national firms of the producing countries.

Again corporate characteristics seem to be controlling. Following a cycle which Raymond Vernon has described in detail,[13] firms typically develop a product in their home base in an advanced industrial country and only move outward from it as they are forced to by economic pressure. Thus opportunities to capitalize on lower natural resource or labor costs abroad, which may appear to offer clear-cut economic advantages, are not immediately seized. They are accepted in time with considerable help from competitive pressure; but as Vernon observes, this is a late stage in the cycle, and considering the relatively early stage of the operations of many multinational firms, it is not surprising that the return-flow process is just beginning to emerge.

There are good reasons to expect that multinational firms will increasingly participate in the reverse flow of resources back to the advanced industrial nations. In the view of some economists, emphasis on expansion of exports of manufactured goods from the less developed countries utilizing their comparative advantage in

[13] Raymond Vernon, "International Investment and International Trade in the Product Cycle," loc. cit.

labor resources is essential for their economic progress. Advocating this point, Hal Lary cites a fourfold increase in these exports from 1953 to 1964.[14] He feels that the force of the economic differentials behind this rise and the initiative of the businessmen involved will carry it ahead. Indications that multinational firms are likely to participate actively in the process are found in their growing procurement of electronic and other products in Japan and the recent establishment of Mexican subsidiary factories along the border to serve U.S. markets.

The extent to which this involvement is carried, however, will be limited by the characteristics of the multinational corporations. They are unlikely to enter actively into the overseas manufacture of products where their primary skill capabilities are not of great value. The major portion of the growth of exports from the less developed countries should logically be in low-skill, high-labor content products which would not by this criterion be appropriate for the international firm. However, there is still room for considerable growth of trade of the nature suggested above in which a modest but critical skill component is combined with a large labor input. Thus multinational corporations will probably take a greater interest in the flow of labor resources in various forms in years to come.

The flow of capital resources is a somewhat different story. The differential pattern has generally been in the same direction as the evolution of the multinational corporation. That is, the advanced countries led by the United States have had greater supplies of capital, and there has been a consistent outward flow of capital from these countries. The multinational corporations have participated in this process, the outflow of U.S. direct private investment averaging $2.3 billion per year from 1960 to 1967. But several factors have limited the flow. There has been some pressure from the U.S. government on its companies to limit capital outflow to help reduce the balance-of-payments deficit. Host governments, especially in many developing countries, have limited inflow of capital by encouraging or requiring joint ventures in which much of the capital for new enterprises is supplied by local investors. But probably the most important cause has been the conservative

[14] Hal B. Lary, "Trade of the LDC's," *Columbia Journal of World Business,* Summer, 1966, p. 76.

financial philosophy noted earlier which is dominant in most multi-national corporations. Characteristically they look upon capital outflows as a means to an end, not an end in itself. That is, they tend to invest such capital as they require to implement their market development strategy which typically means enough to establish a controlling equity base. The balance of their financial needs is then obtained from banks or other local sources. They do not, therefore, invest as much capital as they could abroad.

The use of local capital is sometimes defended by conventional financial criteria. The concept of using leverage to magnify earnings from a limited equity base is common in domestic operations and is equally appropriate in international business. Thus, where it is possible to improve earnings by borrowing from local banks or selling bonds, limiting export of capital has a certain fundamental justification. However, this argument seems doubtful in light of the generally higher interest rates abroad. On a strictly financial return basis, it would be better for most multinational firms to borrow in their parent country and transmit the capital abroad. In fact, most of the large U.S. companies which have issued bonds in Europe since 1964 have paid interest rates of 1 percent or more above what would have been required at home. This is generally accepted as one of the costs of the U.S. program necessary to ease the balance-of-payments problem but not a desirable one in the eyes of some of the corporations which have been historically more astute in maximizing financial returns.

But the emphasis on use of local capital in many companies goes well beyond the normal concepts of maximizing return through use of leverage. Because subsidiaries are part of larger corporate entities, they are not necessarily subject to the same capital structure constraints as are proper for independent firms. It is safe, therefore, to load them up with much higher debt ratios than would be proper for the company as a whole. For example, the study by the National Industrial Conference Board cites a case of a new subsidiary which started operations with $9.5 million of its total $12 million capital in various forms of debt, a large portion of it from local capital sources.[15] In most companies, the bulk of the local capital is borrowed because of the preference for maxi-

[15] Judd Polk et al., *U.S. Production Abroad and the Balance of Payments*, *op. cit.*, p. 97.

mum ownership control. But in a number of companies the desire to minimize U.S. capital input has been a major factor encouraging the joint-venture approach, at least with minority equity capital from local partners and sometimes with majority local participation.

The wisdom of this strategy may be questioned in terms of the basic economic differentials. The companies are apparently passing up an opportunity to profit by the transmission of a resource which they could readily control, except where government regulations intervene. In many cases, their policies contribute to the growth of other channels of capital flow. Some of these are specialized financial institutions in the private sector like banks and investment houses to whom the typical industrial firm may readily defer as more competent for the task. But to a substantial degree the overseas capital flow especially to the less developed countries has had to be handled by public institutions, and this, in turn, has fostered the public sector in the host countries, a situation not favorable to the long-run interests of the multinational firms. Nonetheless, the general philosophy of the firms has a sound basis. The financial risks of overseas operations are considerable, including devaluations, blocked currencies, and the like. Although many companies are quite competent in financial management, this is not their main mission, and there is always the possibility that financial losses may seriously impair their basic production-marketing role.

COUNTRY DECISIONS

The significant feature of decisions on countries to which resources are transmitted is the pattern of location of investments noted earlier with companies emphasizing large markets and low-risk countries and minimizing commitments in smaller markets and those with high risks (see Figure 2.2). This is a natural corollary of the priority given to market position and the financial conservatism among managements. Although this pattern applies generally to multinational firms, there are considerable variations in specific country decisions because of differences in the situation of individual companies.

The farm tractor situation in Turkey in the mid-1950s is illustrative.[16] The Turkish government was putting considerable pressure on companies importing tractors to undertake local manufacturing, offering them a protected market and other forms of support. The major firms like International Harvester consistently declined because their manpower and capital were fully occupied in development of larger and less risky markets. In doing so, they were taking a chance on losing all or a good part of their market position in Turkey if another firm accepted, but on balance they felt that was better than dissipating their resources on a minor market —and logically a number of other small markets where similar pressures for local production existed or where it is anticipated soon might.

Minneapolis-Moline, however, accepted and started a factory in collaboration with various Turkish interests. M-M at the time was competitively weak in the United States, and it had only minor foreign operations. The Turkish venture seemed to offer an opportunity to build a position in a promising market protected from the competition of the major firms which the company would have to meet directly if it were to try to start manufacture in Europe or even key Latin American countries like Brazil or Mexico. The Turkish factory encountered major problems, and Minneapolis-Moline subsequently withdrew from the farm equipment business in the United States. But these developments notwithstanding, at the moment the Turkish factory may well have been a strategically sound vehicle for M-M to transmit such resources as it could command.

Aside from such variations in the position of individual companies, the main options in country decisions depend upon the structure of operations to be discussed next. That is, the extent to which a company will attempt to transmit resources to a country will depend to a considerable degree on the types of arrangements which it is willing to consider to accomplish the transmission process.

[16] Details of this situation are given in John Fayerweather, "The International Harvester Export Company," *Management of International Operations,* McGraw-Hill Book Company, New York, 1960. pp. 133–159; and Richard D. Robinson, "Minneapolis-Moline in Turkey," *Cases in International Business,* Holt, Rinehart and Winston, Inc., New York, 1962, pp. 78–99.

METHODS OF TRANSMISSION

The dominant methods for the transmission of resources are exports and overseas manufacture by subsidiaries in which the parent firm has a controlling interest. In recent years there has been a substantial growth in the number of joint ventures in which multinational firms have a minority position, licensing agreements with independent host-nation firms, and management contracts under which multinational firms run operations, often owned by governmental bodies abroad. But the export, controlled-manufacture structure is still preferred by the great majority of companies primarily because it permits them to function essentially according to their custom with full management control of operations.

There is much to be said for this preference in light of the long-term record of success of the integrated business firm in industrial society. But in the present international context, the pattern may be challenged on logical grounds. A pattern which has proved optimal within one set of environmental conditions may not be optimal in the quite different international environment. The adaptation to host-nation environmental variables, which will be emphasized in subsequent chapters, is quite relevant to the present discussion. The adaptation process should certainly extend into the basic pattern of company activities if that is desirable, and in many instances a case for change can be made. For example, Richard D. Robinson, a forceful advocate of greater flexibility in overseas strategies, argues:

> Because of their domestic concentration on the manufacture and export of merchandise, most nonservice organizations do not see themselves in the business of selling services. Yet, every manufacturer has a number of valuable services that he could sell if he chose, specifically, management skills, marketing skills. . . . There is reason to believe that in many foreign markets, the return to be realized from the sale of services, valuable rights, used machinery, and investible funds (for debt or equity in the portfolio sense) may be substantially greater than the profit to be earned on the export of goods or the return to be generated by direct investment.[17]

[17] Richard D. Robinson, *International Management,* Holt, Rinehart and Winston, Inc., New York, 1967, p. 19.

We must consider as valid variables in the determination of methods of transmission both the differences between domestic business and international business, like greater distance and currency relationships, and the nature of the host-nation societies and their nationalism and national interests, which will be considered in the next two chapters. The analysis at this stage must, therefore, be regarded as partial, with discussion of key aspects of the strategy to be resumed in subsequent chapters.

The partial analysis of methods of transmission considers the issue in the context of the pattern of resource differentials and corporate characteristics which has been outlined in the present chapter. Two elements of this pattern seem most pertinent.

First, there must be a presumption that for different resource differentials, different transmission structures may be *efficient.* For example, in one case the only superior resource outside a country may be an element of technology, there being adequate natural resources, labor, capital, and other skills. In such a situation, a simple licensing arrangement between a multinational firm and a local manufacturer has an apparent logic. There is already a substantial amount of licensing of patents among companies of the advanced industrial nations and to a lesser degree those in other countries, so the question here is simply one of how far an established practice should be expanded. In another situation, a country may be deficient only in technological and managerial skills so that a management contract apparently fits. This type of arrangement is still relatively rare today. Without for the moment considering the suitability of alternatives by internal criteria, these external variables provide an underlying logic for a flexibility of approach which argues against the tendency of many companies to advocate one or another approach for universal application. Approaches in which the major emphasis is on transmitting those resources with the most favorable differentials or which are most suitable for corporate characteristics deserve careful attention as maximizing the efficiency of the strategy.

Second, there is the problem of achievement of the prime objective of market penetration where export or controlled subsidiary operations are precluded by government regulations, excessive risks, or other conditions. This factor has been the main reason for the development of a large portion of the departures from the standard pattern. When companies find they cannot exploit a market by their desired approach, they have frequently accepted joint ventures, licensing, or management contracts as alternatives. This reluctant acceptance is quite a different matter, however, from the deliberate choice of alternatives which a few companies have followed and which is a possibility for more. The critical question is whether, given the financial conservatism of most managements, it might be better as a matter of desired policy to achieve the prime objective of transmission of skills through limited commitment arrangements in those countries where financial risks are significant and perhaps in all countries.

Two considerations both bearing on the *effectiveness* of the transmission process would appear to be controlling in this question. First, there is the importance attached to integrated organizational control over the transmission process. Both the governments and businessmen of countries importing skills often tend to underestimate the complexity of skills and the problems of effectively acquiring them, a problem which is brought out clearly, for example, in Ashok Kapoor's penetrating study of licensing agreements in India.[18] This is a key factor in their advocacy of arrangements like joint ventures and licensing in which the role of the multinational corporation is limited to making information available with a modest instructional and advisory service. The skill-supplying firm, on the other hand, typically feels that the skills can be transferred more effectively if it has a close and intimate control over the operations in which they are employed, and furthermore, that there are certain aspects of skills which are so intimately tied to the corporation that they cannot be transferred separately. This view has support in the detailed study of management contracts undertaken by Peter Gabriel.[19] He finds that the management contract has considerable merit precisely because it does permit full integration of the multinational corporation with the skill transmission process even though there may be no financial commitment.

[18] Ashok Kapoor, "Foreign Collaboration in India," *The Patent, Trademark and Copyright Journal of Research and Education,* Summer, 1966, pp. 230–231, 235–236.

[19] Peter P. Gabriel, *The International Transfer of Corporate Skills,* Harvard Graduate School of Business Administration, Boston, Mass., 1966, p. 61.

Michael Yoshino's study of relations between American and Japanese executives in 50-50 joint ventures provides further confirmation of the difficulty of transmitting skills in nonintegrated organizations.[20] He observed that the majority of Americans "simply accept Japanese managerial practices," even though many of the Japanese apparently were interested in acquiring at least some degree of advanced American know-how. The problem stemmed from several causes, including the ambiguity of the role of the Americans as representatives of part owners, their relative isolation from the Japanese who, because of their culture and their prior association in the Japanese parent, formed a close-knit group, and their doubts about ability to reform Japanese management practices in the short term of their assignment. To some degree these problems would also exist in controlled subsidiaries, but they would be substantially reduced. Thus practical observation apparently confirms the logical conclusion that an integrated organization will be most effective in transmission of skills.

Second, there is the element of continuity of market position which is fundamental to the objectives of the corporation. This, as Gabriel points out in his study, is the really vital distinction between the management contract and the controlled subsidiary, the former having a definite time limit after which the company is quite likely to lose its participation in the market.[21] Although not so clear-cut, the same possibility is ever present in both licensing and minority positions in joint ventures. In both cases a firm may find that those controlling the enterprise in the host country will exclude them from the business at some time in the future.

These two considerations would seem to provide a sound basis for the general corporate preference for a controlling position in its foreign ventures. The employment of the alternative structures then would stand as a second choice when circumstances justify it. The determination of when they are justified would depend upon a considered judgment in each case of the potentials of a market, the possibilities that it may be tapped through other preferable means in the foreseeable future and the availability of corporate resources for other purposes. And in the background, shaping the

---

[20] Michael Y. Yoshino, "Administrative Attitudes and Relations in a Foreign Culture," *MSU Business Topics*, Winter, 1968, pp. 59–66.

[21] Gabriel, *op. cit.*, p. 95.

government actions which have much to do with both the regulations and the risks which force the hand of management, are host country nationalism and national interests which will be examined in Chapter 4.

SUMMARY

In this chapter the first major component of the conceptual framework for the strategy of the multinational firm has been formulated around the role of the firm in transmission of economic resources among nations. Three main groups of factors which compose the basic constraints on the way in which the firm performs this role have been described. Differentials in the supply-demand relationships of resources among countries provide the fundamental economic pressures for the movement of resources, and thus the primary logics for the opportunities open to the multinational firm. Assorted government actions distort the resource-differential relationships in various ways so that the actual pattern of opportunities open to the firm differs considerably from that which would result if free economic forces prevailed. The third group of factors are the characteristics of the multinational firm, notably the prevalent concern with long-term market penetration and conservative capital investment policies.

The interaction of the pattern of opportunities and corporate characteristics has been traced in three key aspects of corporate strategy. First, in the types of resources transmitted, primary emphasis is typically attached to transmission of skills, a strategy related to the combination of substantial differentials among countries and to the suitability of the firm for international skill transmission. On the other hand, although significant differentials also exist in capital and labor, certain characteristics of the multinational firm have not been conducive to strategies emphasizing their transmission. Second, in selection of countries to which resources are transmitted, the opportunities seized are determined as much by factors of internal corporate concern like financial conservatism as by the strength of the resource differentials. Third, in the selection of methods of transmission the prevailing patterns of resource differentials combined with country environmental conditions suggest possible variations of strategies ranging from exports through controlled manufacturing subsidiaries to licensing and management contracts. The corporate characteristics are found, however, to limit substantially the optimal strategies, the emphasis on long-term market penetration and growth typically exerting strong pressure for methods in which continuity of control is maintained. In important aspects of strategy determination, especially as to methods of transmission, it was noted that additional environmental factors are critical variables; and to incorporate them into the conceptual framework, we therefore go on to analysis of relations between the multinational firm and host societies.

Chapter Three
Relations with Host Societies

The transmission of resources in response to economic differentials among nations discussed in the preceding chapter provides the initial logic for the activities of the multinational firm. This function in turn leads inevitably to the second basic cross-border process, the interaction of the firm with foreign societies. The resource transmission process is in itself a form of interaction with the host society. But it is limited essentially to economic interchanges. We must go on to consider the other types of interactions with the host society into which the multinational firm is thrust by this initial economic impetus. Sometimes the contact is superficial as when a company sells to a foreign importer with only a few brief written communications required. More often, however, for the typical multinational firm the interactions are numerous and penetrating as it manages full-scale manufacturing subsidiaries within host societies. Thus the conceptual framework for the strategies of the firm must deal with this wide range of the relations between its activities and the societies within which it attempts to function.

The central issue proposed for this phase of the conceptual framework is the choice between conformity and innovation. In practical terms one can define two strategy postures open to the firm. "A company must adapt itself to conditions in the countries where it operates." "A multinational firm should try to do business in different ways, for one of its major strengths lies in its ability to bring something new into foreign countries." Both of these postures are readily accepted as sound. But it is equally apparent that they inherently run in opposite directions, so by themselves they are inadequate as a basis for management decisions. In some phases of life, conformity is obviously appropriate—respect for

51

local religious codes for example. In others, innovation may be quite clearly sound—introduction of improved medical products for example. But between these extremes there is a vast gray area in which the choice between conformity or innovation is by no means obvious.

The role of the multinational firm in the transmission of resources provides a fundamental guideline as to the types of relations which it should have with the host society. The successful achievement of the transmission process entails change in various forms. Sometimes the change is imperceptible—the modest increment to national capital, for example, which comes when a multinational firm buys a minority interest in a local firm. But in some types of resource transmission, notably the transfer of skills, change in the prevailing nature of the host society may be substantial. We may, therefore, take as an initial component of the strategy of relations with the host society that an objective of innovation will be adopted where change in the host society is essential to achievement of specific forms of resource transmission.

But between the adoption of this objective and the fixing of actual strategy must lie some determination as to feasibility. As was indicated in the previous chapter, the nature of the host society is a critical variable in determining which resources may be effectively transmitted. The conceptual framework must, therefore, embody an approach to analyzing the feasibility of achievement of whatever changes are required for the resource transmission. The outputs from this analysis will then serve as guidelines both for the strategies as to resource transmission and for relations with the host society. In the latter, innovation will be attempted where transmission of resources is determined as feasible in terms of both internation relationships and receptivity of the host society. As a corollary, it may be presumed that in other phases of its activities the firm will seek to conform to the host society to achieve maximum acceptability and thus facilitate the transmission process.

Although it might be adequate to take the resource transmission process as the point of departure for analyzing relations with host societies, a different frame of reference is also pertinent—the concept of the cross-cultural change agent. Since the beginnings of civilization individuals and groups moving from one social group to another have contributed to the transmission of *culture* in its broadest sense of man-made ideas, attitudes, and practices. Early traders played a critical role in passing on not only material goods but assorted social traits from one society to another. Missionaries have actively spread religious ideas. In many ages migrants driven out of their parent societies by ethnic, religious, or other problems or seeking greater opportunities elsewhere have introduced into the societies they joined elements of their former way of life.

The multinational firm fits readily into this picture. It and the parent country nationals who may be brought along to staff local units are generically similar to the other types of cross-cultural change agents observed over the course of time. Thus, though many of its innovative actions are undoubtedly related to the resource transmission process, tying its full innovation role to that function seems too limited a view. Reference to the cross-cultural change-agent concept accepts the possibility that some of the innovations cannot be attributed directly to specific resource differentials. It may be that when future research studies have exhaustively examined the various innovative influences exerted by multinational firms abroad, we will find that all can be traced in one way or another to some form of resource transmission. Pending availability of such studies, however, it is sound to recognize the somewhat different frame of reference of the cross-cultural change agent in the present analysis. In effect, it identifies the multinational firm as a displaced or migrant social entity which carries with it assorted elements of its parent culture. In the process of adapting to its new home, it will to some degree conform to the local ways and to some degree it will attempt to perpetuate its former ways and to convert those around it to follow them as well.

The addition of the cross-cultural change-agent concept to that of the resource transmission process adds a new perspective to the motivations in the relations of the multinational firm with host societies. But it would not appear to alter appreciably the critical analytical problem underlying strategy planning in this area—namely, the determination of the feasibility of innovation. Thus the approach to which this chapter is devoted is essentially applicable, regardless of which frame of reference is employed.

The analytical approach in this chapter will be confined to the relation of innovation to the internal structure of the host society. The next chapter will deal with the special aspects of the receptivity of societies to change efforts as they relate to the attitudes of nationalism and national interest interacting with the multinational firm as a foreign entity.

BUSINESS AND SOCIETY

The essence of the concepts developed in this chapter is the inter-relation of business with the structure of society and the nature of change in components of society. A few fundamental concepts drawn from the social sciences will set the stage for this discussion. Over the centuries men have organized themselves into groupings or societies of progressively broader character—families, tribes, small regional units, and now, most commonly, nations within which common patterns of life prevail. These patterns are typically described as institutions or systems and are classified according to their central purpose. Men in all societies

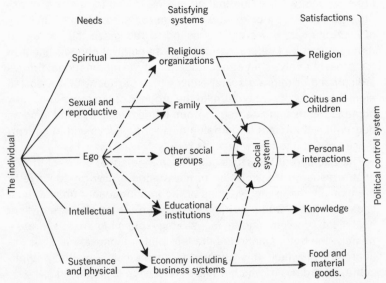

Figure 3.1 The needs of the individual and the systems satisfying them.

have just a few basic needs, and the systems they have evolved are directed toward serving these needs. Thus, as shown in Figure 3.1, spiritual needs are met by religious organizations, sexual and reproductive needs by the family system, intellectual needs by educational institutions, sustenance and physical needs by the economic system including business, and ego needs (chiefly love, status, and security) both by essentially social organizations (e.g., a fraternal association) and by the social interactions associated with the other institutions (e.g., the work group in a factory). There is also the political system which serves a control function in guiding the other systems for the benefit of the members of the society.

Within these systems men are able to function in a reasonably effective and orderly manner by virtue of the existence of two types of established and integrated networks of relationships, one economic and the other personal. The economic network involves the interrelation of the resources of society—natural resources, labor, skills, and capital. These resources are present in a society in varying quantities and qualities, and the demands for them form a particular pattern at a given time. The economic system provides the means for allocation of the resources and direction of economic effort. In completely free economies, most of this allocation and direction is accomplished by independent price and monetary mechanisms. In a highly controlled economy it may be determined by government decisions, though still typically with much use of monetary measures in the processes of planning and exchange. Thus the monetary measures present in a society are typically indicators of the relative utilities and supplies of resources as determined in the society, and the assortment of exchanges which take place on the basis of them keep the society functioning— differences in wages attracting people into particular jobs according to need and productivity, levels of interest encouraging appropriate volumes of investment, and so on. As any observer of the modern world knows, the monetary measure system often functions inadequately. For example, in Brazil the inflationary spiral induced by fiscal problems has resulted in many distortions in price relationships. But despite malfunctions, the system is in being and does provide for the continuity of societies.

The personal network of relationships accommodates the needs of a society made up of human beings rather than robots. It is composed of integrated patterns of roles, expectations, values, and sanctions. Each individual as he operates within each system has a certain position or role, for example, as a priest or a customer or a student. Over the years the society will have evolved a set of expectations for the conduct of the individual in each role—how he is to lead, whom he is to respect, how much he should know, etc. It will also have a system of values which will guide the conduct of people telling them what is right and wrong, what is most desirable, and so on. And there will be some code of sanctions which disciplines the functioning of the system meting out punishments and rewards according to how well people satisfy the established pattern of roles, expectations, and values, ranging all the way from jail terms for gross offenders to minor rebuffs like a curt response to an impolite question and praise or material benefits for those who perform correctly.

This combination of roles, expectations, values, and sanctions is essential to a society because it permits people to act for the most part according to tradition and habit with confidence that they will be effective and that others will be proceeding in the same direction. By the same token it is vital for the perpetuation of the society as a whole. Because the individual aspects have over time evolved as an integrated, interdependent whole, the society is able to hold together and move in a purposeful manner.

Business is a basic component of this structure. It composes a major part of the economic system, providing the mechanism through which most goods and services reach the population wherever private enterprise is accepted. Furthermore, as shown in Figure 3.2, it is closely related to the other systems. The religious system propagates values and sanctions which affect the conduct of business. The family system is also a source of values, and its characteristics bear on business in other ways such as nepotism. The educational system affects business in both the extent and the type of intellectual development people receive throughout the society—its customers, its employees, government officials who control its operations, and so on. The social system is yet another source of values and sanctions, the interactions in business life being a major part of the social activities of people. Finally, one of the prime functions of the political system is direction of the economy, including the business system.

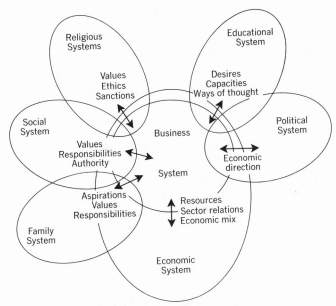

Figure 3.2 Interaction of systems of society. Schematic diagram; only some interactions are shown.

This picture of the components of the society is quite sketchy in its details, but it is adequate to make the key point insofar as the present analysis is concerned—namely, that the individual aspects of each country are interdependent parts of an interrelated whole. In considering the problem of conformity or innovation with respect to any situation, therefore, the multinational firm is not dealing with independently determined elements of society but rather with elements whose nature is in large part dependent upon any number of other elements. Thus it is apparent that conformity-innovation decisions must be based on an understanding of the functioning of the surrounding society so that the business policies and practices adopted will effectively integrate with the assortment of environmental elements. This same observation can, of course, be made about purely domestic management, for every business must fit its methods to its environment. But in relative or practical terms there is a major difference arising from the impetus for the multinational firm to actively seek the introduction of changes from outside the established system of the society.

DIFFERENCES IN RELATIONSHIPS AMONG SOCIETIES

To amplify the concepts outlined above, it will be helpful to illustrate them by describing some of the main dimensions of the economic and personal relationships within societies with which international business is concerned.

Notable on the *economic* side are income-structure, compensation-structure, and capital-labor relationships. The *income structures* of societies vary between the extremes shown in Figure 3.3. Type A represents the very undeveloped economies with the great majority of the people at the low end of the income scale, a small middle class, and a few quite wealthy people. Type B typifies the highly industrialized societies in which the bulk of the population falls in a relatively affluent middle class, with small numbers at both the bottom and top ends of the income scale. A number of economic relationships are influenced heavily by the income structure. In the type A society the buying capacity among the masses is limited to a few staples and minor luxuries; so the effective demand for most consumer durables and many other products is found only among the small middle- and upper-class groups. A few typical consequences of this sort of structure are packaging of mass consumption items like chewing gum in very small units within the buying power of the poor; emphasis on luxury lines of

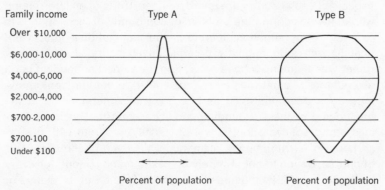

Figure 3.3 Sample income structures of societies.

durable goods with high margins to maximize profit from the upper class; and distribution and advertising methods designed to pinpoint coverage of one economic level, either the elite or the lower class, because their characteristics are so different. The closer one approaches the type B structure, the more emphasis there is on developing products suitable for the mass middle class, with less attention to the special demands of the upper and lower extremes. Likewise, advertising and distribution methods are directed more toward complete coverage of the market without distinction as to economic level.

The *compensation structure* is the other side of the coin related to manpower resources, skills, and productivity. In the type A society the great majority of the people are typically engaged in agriculture where they have low productivity due to small land units and unprogressive methods—lack of fertilizers, ineffective cultivation, and the like. The balance of the low-income groups are urban masses who are for the most part either unemployed or low-skill laborers. The relatively small portions of the population possessing the bulk of the technical, managerial, and entrepreneurial skills are found in the middle- and upper-income groups. Although this sort of compensation structure is disturbing by humanitarian standards, it reflects appropriately the economic contributions of the various groups and provides incentives in a constructive direction. That is, an individual with skills in such a society contributes relatively much more to economic output than a member of the low-skill masses, and the existence of high economic rewards encourages people at the lower end to develop skills which are badly needed. In the type B societies the disparity in economic contribution has been narrowed by mass education and the broad dissemination and organization of skills in agriculture and industry, though a considerable span of compensation does of course remain. The obvious relevance of the compensation relationships lies in the wage and salary structure established by a company, but it affects other aspects of business. For example, in type A societies the scarcity of skilled people and the low wages and unemployment among the unskilled encourage firms to avoid layoffs, thus reinforcing practices which have social support as will be indicated below.

The *capital-labor* relationship also relates to availability and productivity. In the less developed countries as compared with the advanced nations, capital is less available, and labor at lower-skill levels is more plentiful relative to needs. Indicative of these differences we find interest rates are higher in the less developed countries, and wage rates are higher in the advanced countries. Putting the two together, we see that the ratio of cost of capital to cost of labor is higher in the less developed societies. This type of relationship bears most directly on the processes and technology employed in business. In the less developed countries it favors the use of low-investment, labor-intensive methods. The opposite tendency is favored as one moves up the scale of industrial development of nations. But to illustrate the complexity of the effects of various elements in a society, it is worth noting that the approach in less developed countries can be quite different because of other relationships. For example, companies have on occasion used quite automated processes requiring high investments because they found it easier to manage a few high-wage, high-skilled workers than to deal with larger numbers of people with low skills, sometimes because of irresponsible labor unions dominating the latter. This illustration simply emphasizes that the determination of policies which will fit best in a given society depends upon an understanding of all of the relationships in the society, not just a few obvious ones.

Turning to the *personal* relationship side, we find a much more variegated picture. There does seem to be some relation between level of economic development and cultural, social, and political characteristics. However, the human element has played such a strong part in the historical evolution of these characteristics that the nature of the personal relationships varies greatly even among countries at similar levels of economic achievement. Of the assortment of relationships which compose the full web of the structure of a host society, six are especially pertinent to the interaction of foreign business with the society: groupings of people, interpersonal obligations, authority systems, value systems, interbusiness relationships, and politico-economic controls.

The earliest *groupings of people* stemmed naturally from the reproduction process and elemental self-protection and subsistence needs. As human life became more sophisticated, it was natural that the family should remain the fundamental unit onto which people would attempt to graft new activities. Thus we find in many societies, especially those at early stages of development, that a large portion of the personal relationships are built around familial ties. Very frequently some version of the *extended family* (or clan or tribe) became an important unit with even quite distant relatives functioning on a fairly close and continuing basis. In such societies people do have other group affiliations, but they are not numerous and are not considered as important to their lives. A quite different structure is found in some of the more economically advanced countries. The family is still a significant unit but only in the limited nuclear form (husband, wife, and children). A large portion of the individual's activities take place in a multiplicity of groupings, ranging from business firms to religious organizations, to political parties, to social clubs, any of which may be important enough to him to rival his family ties.

The nature of personal groupings affects business at many levels. The policies of a firm may be quite different if it is essentially an arm of a family unit rather than a widely owned independent economic unit. The economic objectives of the family, stemming from its other activities and even such noneconomic considerations as family pride, may be determining factors, whereas the independent firm is better able to act on the basis of its separately determined objectives. In a number of aspects of operating, such as procurement and selling, managers imbued with strong extended-family orientation are likely to exert their efforts and develop relationships in the direction of family ties to a greater degree than men from societies in which multiple affiliations prevail.

In employment practices the dominance of family ties leads naturally to nepotism. Hiring relatives is found in all societies. The difference in the family-oriented societies lies in the tendency to give much greater weight to family affiliation in selection as compared to technical proficiency or other qualifications. Because nepotism is often viewed very critically in some advanced nations in which multinational managers are raised, it may be well to pause here for a moment to emphasize the point that each characteristic of a society has a logical place within that society. Nepotism is frequently found where general standards of business morality are not high and where the supply of competent managers is quite limited.

These conditions provide a justification for emphasis on employing relatives because family codes can enforce morality and family loyalty can attract and hold managers. Thus under some circumstances nepotism is sound by both social and economic standards, even if it results in some sacrifice of managerial qualifications.

The system of *interpersonal obligations* in a society stems in part from the groupings of people and in part from the relations between groups. Variations are found among countries in both the patterns of obligations and their strength. Two illustrations will suggest the range of variations.

In the United States the multiple-group affiliations of the individual carry with them some obligations to others; so the general pattern is quite wide. On the other hand, few obligations seem to have great strength or durability: children leave home early and take little responsibility for their parents, compared to that in many countries; workers do the job for which they are paid, but they manifest little company loyalty and move on to other companies quite readily; consumers shift their buying from store to store and product to product with ease; and so on.

Japan composes a quite different picture. Traditional Japanese society was rigidly structured including a well-defined code of obligations for almost every situation—parent-child, worker-employer, businessman-emperor, etc. Though some elements of these obligations have faded, much still remains. Thus, for example, when a young man is hired for management in a Japanese firm, it is typically assumed that lifetime obligations have been assumed on both sides—the company assures the manager a job and steady increases in status and pay, and the man, in turn, remains in loyal employment in the firm. This type of paternalism is perhaps stronger in Japan than elsewhere, but to a degree it is common in many other countries. By the same token, in Japan and other societies one finds quite strong ties between housewives and small food merchants. Lower- and middle-class women tend to shop frequently, and they develop regular relationships with a small group of neighborhood merchants. It is hard to determine to what extent their actions are the result of simple habit, of desire for regular social intercourse, and of sense of obligation to support the merchants who provide a convenient service. But as a practical matter, a strong bond exists, which is a controlling factor distribution plans.

Authority systems are also largely a component of the groupings of individuals. The chief differences among societies are along the range between authoritarian-autocratic systems and democratic-participative systems. The former is the traditional pattern whose origins can be traced back to the way of life of primitive man. In simple societies it seems to have been natural for the strongest and wisest to achieve control and, with varying degrees of consultation with others, to make and enforce decisions within the group. In any case, we find today authoritarian patterns still well established in important sectors of life of many countries including the family, religion, education, government, and business. Democratic patterns are generally dominant in the United States, parts of Europe, and some other areas like Canada and Australia. In a number of countries there is a mixed picture, with authoritarian systems dominant in some groups and democratic ones in others. In much of Latin America, for example, democratic concepts find a striking manifestation in student participation in important decisions, including faculty appointments in some public universities. On the other hand, authoritarian patterns persist for family life and for the student-teacher relationship within the classroom.

The obvious relevance of authority systems for business lies in the pattern of internal management. Where authoritarian relationships prevail, the multinational firm is likely, at least to some degree, to find it must relate itself to expectations of local employees along those lines, even though its expatriate managers may have come from societies where democratic approaches were common. But the authority system bears on other aspects of business. In marketing, it is important in planning promotion and other activities to know whether it is the husband or the wife who makes purchasing decisions, and for industrial goods whether it is the president or the purchasing manager. In negotiating with governments on all sorts of problems, it is necessary to know whether lower-level bureaucrats have true delegated authority or whether decisions can only be made by cabinet ministers or in some cases by the chief of state.

The question of *value systems* brings us into a different order of

Values are pervasive mental attitudes
/f the standards of the individual as to what
/ or bad, desirable or undesirable. Because
1 of social, religious, educational, and other
.rs, they form a very mixed picture around the
ι is difficult to generalize. Thus it is practical
he. y a few interesting variations in values to indicate the ιυ. may take. One variation important to business is
the respect accorded by societies to different occupations. In most
traditional societies the highest prestige was given to scholars or
warriors or government leaders, with business people typically
falling fairly low on the scale. The low esteem of business arose
from a lack of appreciation for the contributions of business, the
image of the businessman as one who profited at the expense of
the main body of the population and the relatively weak power
position of business vis-a-vis the governing elites. Even in most
European countries, this low valuation of business careers per-
sists, with only a few societies fitting the U.S. pattern in which
business is at least reasonably close to other ways of life in prestige. All of this, of course, bears heavily on such matters as the type
of personnel who can be recruited into management and the
acceptability and conduct of the businessmen in other circles of
national society.

Another set of values affecting business is the way in which
people view different forms of achievement in life. People attach
various relative weights to material goods, social standing, intellectual accomplishment, power, and so forth. The United States
has often been characterized as a highly materialistic society. However, although the acquisition of material goods is thoroughly approved in the U.S. middle class, it appears that the attainment of social status is more important. Material goods are sometimes
valued more as status symbols indicative of social standing than
for their material benefits (the *nouveau riche* lady perspiring under
a mink stole at a summer concert being a classic case). In some
other countries, on the other hand, ostentatious demonstrations of
material wealth or, in fact, the whole idea of self-generated
achievement is frowned upon. The British are often cited as an
example of a society in which a person is born to a place in the
social hierarchy and expected to stay there. Thus achievement per

se is not to be praised, and status symbols accordingly are not a dominant element in social relations. This type of value affects both marketing decisions and the way in which personnel are managed, for the whole incentive system of business must be geared to the objectives which people feel will have social approval.

Yet another set of values concerns the ways in which people interact, including codes of frankness, courtesy, cooperation, competition, and so on. An extreme but illustrative example of contrast in the combinations of these components observed around the world is seen in differences in the ways of U.S. and Japanese businessmen. Both work in industrialized nations dominated by large firms requiring internal collaboration among managers and extensive external relationships. Yet there are notable differences in the patterns of conduct which are approved by their respective value systems. The American is supposed to be "all business," not wasting time on "nonessentials," and to be frank and precise. The Japanese, on the other hand, devotes a great deal of time in business relationships to pleasantries and other nonbusiness conversation, and he is more concerned with being agreeable than with complete or accurate discussion of business matters. Thus, whereas the American is conditioned to spelling out the full nature of a problem, including both the good and the bad aspects, the Japanese may reveal only part of his knowledge on the matter. Likewise, when the American agrees to a course of action, he is usually doing just that; but the Japanese may be more concerned with being agreeable and not, in fact, have precise intentions as to whether he can or will fulfill the apparent agreement.

A final element of value systems worth noting for its business relevance is the question of honesty. In most societies *honesty* is approved, but what that means in the complex of attitudes composing the value system varies greatly. In the United States a shoplifter or a man who forges checks or takes bribes will not only be prosecuted by the law but will also be looked down upon by his neighbors. Yet thousands of people pad insurance claims or engage in petty income tax evasion by not reporting small sources of income (incidental baby-sitting, for example) with the full knowledge of neighbors, yet with no significant loss of social standing. In many countries, large-scale tax evasion or taking of bribes are commonplace among people who regard themselves as "honest" by the values of their countrymen.

This type of variation again emphasizes the fact that all elements of personal relationships have to be recognized as part of a total societal structure. Whatever the honesty system of a society may be, it is presumably related to and consistent with the other aspects of that society. For example, the mere fact that there is massive tax evasion does not mean that the government has less revenue than it might have, for it presumably can adjust tax rates and other processes to obtain the revenue it needs and the country can afford to pay. More likely it means that the tax load is proportionately heavier on some groups than it might be if tax evasion were not so great. But even this may serve a purpose, for the conditions in the country may be such that the added monetary return for particular activities provided by the tax evasion is necessary to foster these activities—for example, to encourage the wealthy to invest in new industrial operations. By the same token, bribery of government officials is often associated with low salary levels, the bribes providing in effect a means for direct taxation for government services and supplemental compensation of underpaid officials. Whether or not tax evasion and bribery are still suitable for these societies is another question which might be considered as part of the section on change in societies later in the chapter. The only point being stressed here is that absolutes in honesty are no more relevant than any other absolutes in the study of the relationships in a society. The prime consideration is essentially to determine what degrees and forms of honesty are required by the prevailing value system.

The subject of *interbusiness relationships* brings us close to the economic aspects of society, but the personal element in it is strong. The basic issue in these relationships is how a society balances the benefits of competition and collaboration in economic endeavor. Some degree of competition is always beneficial as indicated, for example, by the virtual universality of patent laws which provide a protected incentive for those who develop new products. And collaboration in such matters as joint efforts to develop favorable business legislation has equally common acceptance. But there are many differences among societies which have evolved in other respects. Notable among these is the control of marketing activities.

There seems to be a natural tendency for large industrial firms to seek considerable collaboration to minimize price and volume uncertainty and maximize profit in the marketplace. This tendency was very much in evidence in the United States around the end of the nineteenth century and can be seen in Europe and Japan in the extensive cartelization of business and in less systematic but tangible form in many developing nations. In time, U.S. society decided that substantial limitations on collaboration embodied in the Sherman Antitrust Act and other legislation were desirable.

Other nations have adopted some limitations but for the most part considerably less than the United States. There are differences in their circumstances which bear on the balance they have chosen. For one thing their markets are smaller, so there is less room for competitors to function. In some cases, the economies of scale preclude the efficient operation of enough companies to achieve effective competition. Perhaps more important, there are temperamental differences which are the reason for considering this under the heading of personal relationships. U.S. society has placed high values on economic progress with strong pressures for low costs, low prices, and increased output but relatively lower value placed on the human cost, whether it be in the strain on senior executives or the layoffs of workers in companies which could not survive competition. In other societies these values seem to be reversed. The managerial-entrepreneurial class with support of labor seems more concerned with stabilizing their situation and avoiding competitive pressures and casualties and less anxious to maximize economic progress. Given this outlook, it is quite natural to accept a much greater degree of collaboration than is approved in the United States.

Under *politico-economic controls* fall the assortment of ways in which the people through their political system attempt to guide their economic life. The regulation of interbusiness relationships is part of this as are price controls, investment incentives, ownership of factories, and a host of other government activities. Without delving into the details of any of these, we can discern among societies certain basic patterns or philosophies of politico-economic controls which are most pertinent to our discussion. Again thinking in terms of a spectrum, we find the range runs from virtually full government control to quite free private enterprise. The archetype of the former would of course be a communist state in which the economy is entirely owned and managed by the state. From this we move to countries with varying degrees of state ownership and controls to a relatively few Western nations in which most economic activity is by private companies subject to numerous government regulations, there being no wide-open economies lacking the latter ingredient which would fall at the other extreme of the spectrum.

A number of factors have contributed to these differences in control structures. On the basis of historical experience we may judge that there is a human predisposition toward private enterprise, manifest, for example, in the tenacious resistance to collective farming in Russia. Thus the decision of a society through its political system to exercise collective controls may be presumed to be based on the conclusion that the private system was not in some ways suitable to its situation. This presumption seems to be borne out by the nature of conditions around the world where several elements in different portions have made full reliance of private enterprise questionable. In some countries there were not enough of the right type of entrepreneurs to stimulate economic growth, or they have lacked the essential capital; in others, the risks and problems have been too great a deterrent to entrepreneurs; in still others, there was an apparent need to push the economy in directions which private enterprise was not appropriate to pursue; and in many cases there has been a sense that speed and socially equitable development were best achieved under public controls.

This sketchy survey of economic and personal relationships within societies does not presume to cover all the relationships pertinent to business nor to describe the few which have been mentioned sufficiently to guide the manager in dealing with them.[1]

[1] The reader who wishes to supplement this brief review of the elements of societies and their interrelation may consult several sources. The basic systems of economic and personal relationships are drawn from fundamental economics and sociology which are described in many books (e.g., Paul A. Samuelson, *Economics*, McGraw-Hill Book Company, New York, 1967; and Paul B. Horton and Chester L. Hunt, *Sociology*, McGraw-Hill Book Company, New York, 1964. The variations among these in different countries are best pursued in the small but growing literature of comparative business including J. Boddewyn, *Comparative Management and Marketing*, Scott, Foresman, Chicago, 1968; and R. N. Farmer and B. M. Richman, *Comparative Management and Economic Progress*, Richard D. Irwin, Homewood, Ill., 1965.

Its objective rather has been to provide enough illustrations to give substantive meaning to the concepts of the relation of business to the systems of society and the interrelationship of various societal characteristics. The illustrations, even though presented in sketchy form, clearly show that in many ways operations will be subject to adjustment on the basis of aspects of the local business system, which, in turn, are to some degree controlled by elements of the host-society environment. Sometimes just one element of societal systems will be relevant, but as often as not several inter-related elements exercise influence on a business action.

PROCESS OF CHANGE

In order to determine the feasibility of innovation, we must go beyond the analysis of the interrelation of the elements of societies to a concept of the process of change in the elements. As a starting point, a further dimension must be added to the picture just presented. The integrity and self-perpetuation of the elements of society may imply a simple uniformity, but there is in all societies some diversity in the character of each element. One finds, for example, some variety in the nature of relations within a family or the conduct of businessmen. This variety is induced by the range in personal characteristics of people and lack of uniformities in other circumstances. Within limits a society is able to tolerate variations in the character of each of its elements so long as the tendency in most instances is confined to a narrow range centered about what is called the *norm* of the society as shown in Figure 3.4.[2]

When one considers the question of change in societies, it is helpful to recognize the significance of the characteristics which fall on the outer extremities of Figure 3.4 and the logics of change at work in the process. The infrequent characteristics are of two general types. First, there are those shown at the left of the figure which are for one reason or another not useful to the society.

[2] The term *norm* is used here in the statistical sense of the average or median. It is not to be confused with the use of the term by sociologists to describe a standard according to the value system of a society. In some cases, a characteristic of a society may be a norm by both definitions—for example, when honesty in business relations is both approved and commonly practiced. But for many characteristics there is a norm or prevailing mode which, as used here in the statistical sense, is either not guided by the value system or possibly runs counter to apparent values.

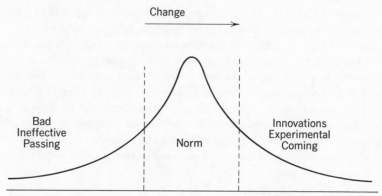

Figure 3.4 Norms, deviants, and change in social systems.

Some are bad like sadistic conduct of a father or poor workmanship by artisans. Others are ineffective or inappropriate to the society as, for example, celibate religious sects like the Shakers who have great difficulty perpetuating themselves. And a substantial group represents passing aspects of the society which linger on, though with decreasing frequency.

Second, there are those characteristics shown at the right which, though not frequent, are definitely useful, representing innovations, experiments, or similar deviations which will in time become established or at least will continue as constructive stimulants to the whole society. The idea of piece rates for factory workers fell into this category when it was first conceived; though initially unusual, it has now become a norm for industrial societies. The concept of the deviant as a useful stimulant is illustrated by the "stormy petrel" type, who emerges as a valuable member of some management groups. Such a type as a norm would result in chaos, but one provocative character in a group can be worth a great deal.

With the deviants from the norm categorized in this manner, the dynamic process is readily incorporated in Figure 3.4 by adding the arrow at the top. Or a third dimension could be added showing the distribution of variations for a particular element of society at subsequent times. It would show some of the deviants on the right, shifting in toward the center to become the norms and some of those on the left, decreasing still more in frequency and being replaced by those close to the current norms. In food retailing in rural sections of the United States for example, a chart a hundred years ago would have shown the norm as the general store run by an individual proprietor, with stores specializing in food being rather infrequent. Thirty years ago the general store would have shifted to the left, becoming a deviant with the store concentrating primarily on food, assuming the status of the norm but with supermarkets appearing here and there. By the 1960s the true general store would have virtually disappeared, and the supermarket would be the norm with various further modernization experiments to the right.

The magnitude of the dimensions both from right to left and in rate of transition through time will vary substantially according to the elements of society and the nature of the societies. In some aspects of life, like recreational interests for example, society tolerates a much wider range of variations than others like religion. Thus the chart for recreational interests of boys in Mexico might show soccer as a norm but with baseball as a rapidly emerging variant and a number of other fairly common alternatives so that the chart would have a rather wide span and an irregular profile. In religious views on the other hand, the vast majority of people would cluster around the norm of Catholicism with a much smaller and narrower band of deviants. By the same token, there are differences in the general tolerance of deviations among societies. Typically the older societies have been the more rigid, with all elements within them held quite close to their norms, and newer societies have had greater tolerance.

The rate of transition typically is related to the range of tolerance in the society. That is, those societies which are fairly rigid in their tolerance of deviations from a norm at any given time are also likely to change slowly. Those which tolerate substantial variations are likely to change more rapidly. However, the rate of change is also subject to other influences, notably from the outside. Especially relevant to this discussion is the influence of the more developed nations on the less developed ones, particularly in business methods. Thus a number of societies which of themselves were quite rigid have been changing fairly rapidly as a result of influence from the United States, Russia, and other countries.

In analyzing and especially in predicting the process of change, one must have some guides as to why change takes place. The most practical concept for this purpose is that the evolution of norms and deviants depends upon their usefulness to the society or, in technical terms, whether they are *functional* or *dysfunctional*. This concept postulates that a particular norm for one element of a society will persist so long as it is functionally the most effective available alternative. When it ceases to serve well and a preferable alternative emerges, it becomes dysfunctional, the alternative taking over as the norm. A large portion of the changes through history certainly fit this general concept; the automobile superseded the horse and buggy when the utility of the former was established by both technological improvements and by economic progress which made it a feasible purchase for the average man; the publicly owned corporation has largely taken the place of the family firm in the more advanced countries because of the greater effectiveness of the corporation in mobilizing large capital requirements for major industrial projects and in building and maintaining the strong managerial organizations required for a dynamic, large enterprise, and so on.

The usefulness criterion is not adequate as a total explanation of the process of change because other causes must be considered, notably the need for sources of initiative to set change in motion which have been greater at some times and in some societies than in others. But it is an essential criterion inasmuch as few dysfunctional variants make substantial progress, and the main thrust of development in societies has been toward useful change. We come down, therefore, to the conclusion that the critical test in the evaluation of the feasibility of an innovation is whether it will be functional or dysfunctional within the evolving elements and systems of the host society.

THE ROLE OF THE MULTINATIONAL FIRM

The foregoing discussion provides the basis for setting forth a conceptual scheme for determining the strategy of the multinational firm in its relations with the internal structure of the host society (as distinguished from the nationalism and national interest aspects to be considered in the next chapter). The special role of the firm as a foreign body within the host society lies in the introduction of innovations, a role which may be considered as part either of its function in the transmission of resources or its activities as a cross-cultural change agent. Thus a primary disposition toward innovation in the strategy is conceptually sound. The critical decisions lie in the determination of the feasibility of innovation. The useful criteria in this determination are (1) whether an innovation fits with the interrelated elements of the host society and (2) whether it will be functionally effective for the society.

To give further meaning to these concepts, we shall indicate some of their practical implications. The main proposition embodied in the concepts is that the multinational firm should be ever anxious to introduce innovations drawn from experience in its home country (or other countries). Though this sort of strategy is inevitably subject to criticisms of chauvinism and even imperialism, with implications for the attitudes to be discussed in the next chapter, it is supported by the logics of the situation. "When in Rome, do as the Romans do" is a nice adage, but it is useful primarily for people like tourists and diplomats whose main objective is to get along well with their hosts. It is of doubtful value as an overall guide for anyone who is going to actively participate in the give-and-take of the life of the society, for the obvious query is, "Can a non-Roman ever hope to be a better Roman than a true Roman?" The answer almost certainly is "no," leading clearly to the conclusion that a strong competitive status for an international company requires departure from local norms either in product design, or in training methods, or in any number of other directions. Furthermore, since the main competence of the multinational firm to innovate must rest on its parent-country experience, it will presumably be most effective if the innovations it attempts are based on that experience. And to further counter the imperialistic implication, this form of innovation represents one of the clear values to the host society of the presence of the firm in its midst. To a substantial degree the firm must conform to the host society if it is to function effectively, but its special strengths both competitively and for the benefit of the host society lie in the innovations it is able to contribute.

The basic guidelines presented here seem conceptually clear and sound, but it will be well to clarify and test them by application to some concrete situations. In the pages which follow, four situa-

tions of varied character and complexity are outlined for this purpose: a product innovation, a change in personnel management,
the introduction of a new marketing institution, and a complex
case involving political-business relations and personal interactions.

1 The Sewing Machine

One of the first of the multitude of new products introduced into
countries by foreign firms was the sewing machine brought to
Europe by Singer in the 1850s. The norm for domestic sewing at
the time was of course the handwork of the housewife, and it re-
mained that for many years. So long as most people were quite
poor and their labor cheap, the investment in a sewing machine
was not economically sound. But for a few more affluent housewives, along with many tailors, seamstresses, etc., the investment
was feasible and the economics of higher productivity proved beneficial. Thus, in time, machine sewing shifted from being a promising deviant to become the norm for home sewing in European
society and now for all but the poorest nations.

There is nothing very subtle about this story, but it is highly relevant because so much of the innovation done by multinational
firms is in the product area, and the economic aspects of product
acceptance are so strong. One can find cultural and other factors
at work in this and similar product changes. For example, in some
societies skilled hand seamstresses have doubtless deplored the
loss of their status to a machine. But by and large, companies
which have introduced laborsaving products which were consistent with the evolution of economic relationships in host societies
have succeeded. They have a natural advantage in doing so because their home-country economy has typically already passed
through the stages of economic development found in host nations, and thus they are skilled in producing goods suitable for
such markets. We find in the multiplicity of such cases, therefore, a
clearly visible confirmation of the general concept of innovation
being feasible and desirable if it fits with the functionally effective
deviations from the norms of the host society.

2 Paternalism and the Personnel Manager

A classic case of cultural innovation revolves around the role of the personnel manager. In major companies in the more advanced societies, the personnel manager is the focal point for many of the personal problems and grievances of workers. The supervisor of course has a role in this aspect of the lives of his subordinates. But consistent with the concepts of organizational specialization, the personnel manager is given the time and responsibility for doing a large part of the job. On the other hand, in the paternalistic systems characteristic of many host nations, the supervisor and quite commonly the senior manager of the plant assume this full function. It is fundamental to the whole structure of paternalism that the organizational leader looks out for all the needs of his people.

One's first reaction to this situation is likely to be that conformity is clearly in order, that an attempt to substitute the personnel manager in part of the role of the supervisor is unwise. By and large this reaction is sound. Paternalistic dependency among workers is usually reinforced by similar relationships throughout the host society—in family, in schools, in church, and in government. A norm of this sort based on pervasive, strong emotional attitudes is not readily altered. Thus a company which attempts to create a structure in which part of the prime paternalistic responsibilities are shifted to someone who is not the leader of the organization risks disruption of worker morale.

However, in terms of the concepts advanced in this chapter the situation requires a careful second look. Paternalism was once the dominant norm in U.S. industry, but it has largely disappeared. Looking at other countries over time, one can clearly discern shifts in the same direction. Changes in the surrounding society provide a logical explanation. Paternalism is related to the economic and educational weakness of workers. As this weakness declines, the logic of dependency declines. By the same token, industrial efficiency is impaired if senior supervisors devote excessive time to personal problems of individual workers. The productivity of the organization as a whole increases as this function is channeled into the specialized hands of the personnel manager.

So it appears that given the commitment of virtually all societies to advancement of the status of workers and greater industrial output, the growing role of the personnel manager will at some point be a functionally effective deviation. The question then becomes not "yes" or "no" but "when" and "how." That is to say, the multinational firm must judge in each host society where paternalism is still the norm just how strong the bases for the norm are and how ready the workers may be for the deviant pattern. Then it must determine what pattern of deviant structure may be feasible, typically following a pattern substantially modified from its home-country norm. For example, a small start may be made by having the personnel manager sit with the senior manager in listening to workers' problems and gradually take an increasing role in dealing with them until the workers begin to look to him rather than the senior manager as the natural person to go to with problems. Note that the innovation in this case is functionally effective but still reasonably consistent with the underlying attitudes fostering paternalism in the individual. No attempt has been made to alter the degree of dependence among the workers. This may change in time. But for the moment the production efficiency objective is achieved by redirecting the dependency.

3   Supermarkets in Less Developed Countries

In 1955 International Basic Economy Corporation opened a supermarket in Venezuela, the first of its kind in Latin America. Since then supermarkets have appeared throughout Latin America and in many other less developed regions. To a degree these stores represent a transfer of retailing methods from the United States, but in considerable part they are new institutions which have evolved out of the changing characteristics of their host societies. For centuries food marketing in less developed countries was dominated by the characteristics of two groups: the impoverished masses who purchased the bulk of the food with primary emphasis on essentials and low prices and the affluent upper class which consumed many types of food with little concern for prices. The needs of these groups were served effectively by small merchants operating out of little stores or more commonly in large open markets with low overhead and minimal labor costs. The lower classes haggled directly with the merchants for their simple needs, and the upper classes sent their servants to shop around among the tradesmen. The small middle class fitted itself into this picture uncomfortably but adequately. The middle-class housewife might be able to afford a servant to do her shopping, but often as not she would go out herself to find the best bargains in the open market, accepting the noise and dirt as part of life.

The notable change in recent years to which the supermarket is geared has been the rapid growth of the middle class along with the availability of greater variety of foods. The story is not, however, simply one of the transfer of a marketing institution developed in middle-class United States to fill comparable middle-class needs elsewhere. The logics of the institution are different.

A crucial element in the success of the supermarket in the United States was the rising cost of labor. The convenience of a large store with a broad product selection and a parking lot has been a factor in its success, but these features could have been provided by another type of store. The unique contribution of the supermarket, especially during its formative period in the Depression period of the 1930s was the efficiency achieved by combining large volume and self-service with consequent low unit labor costs and prices appreciably lower than in smaller, clerk-served stores.

This element is not a major factor in the less developed countries. Labor there is still cheap, and because of their high investment and overhead costs, the prices in supermarkets are generally higher than those of small merchants, especially for fresh foods. Although a simplistic analysis of the evolution of the host societies might have projected the feasibility of introducing a middle-class U.S. retailing institution from the emergence of the middle class, that analysis per se would have been incorrect.

The supermarket is succeeding as an effective deviant from the traditional norm for other reasons centering around convenience and sanitation. The middle-class housewife in the less developed countries is hard pressed for both time and money. In a status-conscious society she is trying hard to stretch the income her husband earns as an engineer or bureaucrat or teacher. So economy is important to her, but that does not mean buying at the place with the lowest price. She may have a servant who can do her shopping, but servants are becoming more expensive as industrialization raises wages; so it costs money to send a maid on a tour of small merchants, and the net cost of buying everything from the supermarket may be less. More commonly, however, the housewife will do much of the shopping herself because choices among the variety of foods available today cannot be delegated to the caliber of maid she can hire. For her the time factor, plus the nuisance of going from merchant to merchant, is a strong incentive favoring one-stop shopping at the supermarket.

The sanitation element provides a decisive push. Modernity and Western standards have become prime cultural values among the new middle class. They want very much to live the life of the housewife of the advanced countries as they see it in magazines, the movies, etc. A prominent aspect of that way of life is cleanliness. So the housewife is increasingly repelled by the dirt and shabbiness of the old stores and street markets and is attracted to the bright, clean supermarkets.

One more feature should be noted to underscore the fact that these supermarkets are not carbon copies of U.S. counterparts. In some less developed countries the stores provide boys to push carts around for shoppers and even to put things in the carts for them. This clearly is a product of status values in societies where manual labor is considered beneath the dignity of people of reasonable social standing. It inevitably adds to the cost of the food, so we can readily conclude that economy beyond a certain point is less important to these people than social status.

4   The Canton Drug Company [3]

The Canton Drug Company had set up a joint venture in Zardin, a Middle Eastern country, with a local businessman, Abdul Baba, and an associate of his, Ali Tabrizi. This move was precipitated by a Zardinian government decree requiring that certain drug products be manufactured in the country. Canton had built a good business in Zardin, relying on imports from the United States sold by a distribution company owned by Mr. Baba. The joint venture, Wadi

---

[3] Summarized by permission from John Fayerweather, *Management of International Operations,* McGraw-Hill Book Company, New York, 1960, pp. 49–55. Original copyright by President and Fellows of Harvard College.

Drug Company, was started with $280,000 capital of which Canton supplied $120,000, Mr. Baba $120,000, and Mr. Tabrizi $40,000. Mr. Baba was generally considered a very able man both in business circles and in politics. He was a member of parliament in the majority party and recognized as a potential prime minister. Mr. Tabrizi was also in parliament in the same party and was employed as an attorney by many local and foreign firms. The chief spokesman for Canton was Thomas Phillips, the Middle Eastern manager who made his headquarters in Zardin.

The venture proceeded well at the outset. Although several companies sought manufacturing licenses, Wadi received full approval for its plans quickly with two other firms obtaining licenses a little later. One of these was entirely owned by a U.S. company and one was a joint effort of European and Zardinian capital. As only a few drugs were to be manufactured, all firms continued to import most of their requirements. An old warehouse was purchased by Wadi and fitted out with obsolete equipment from the U.S. parent which was quite adequate for the simple mixing, tablet making, and bottling operations to be undertaken.

Wadi earned a profit of $110,000 in the first year of operation and the board of directors voted a dividend of the full amount. Mr. Phillips expressed some doubts at this action, but as there was no immediate need for funds he did not feel he had a basis for arguing his point. During the next year the company continued to do well and an interim dividend of $140,000 was proposed in August. Mr. Phillips again objected, feeling some profits should be retained; but as there was still no clear need for funds, he felt unable to press his view, and the dividend was approved. At the end of the year the accounts showed $72,000 of undistributed profits, and Mr. Baba proposed that it be paid out in dividends.

Mr. Phillips felt at this point that there was good reason for retaining profits, and he found that the local auditor, Mr. Iktisat, agreed. Mr. Iktisat prepared a statement pointing out that the old equipment in the plant was rapidly wearing out. Even though 20 percent depreciation was being taken each year, the reserves would not be adequate because inflation in Zardin was running about 20 percent per year. Thus it would be wise to retain the balance of the profits as a reserve for reequipment. Subsequently, Mr. Phillips advised Mr. Baba that Mr. Iktisat concurred in his views, and he was now completely opposed to a further dividend.

The following day Mr. Baba proposed a limited dividend of $30,000. He produced a statement which, he said, Mr. Iktisat had written, suggesting such a dividend. Mr. Baba was not aware of the statement Mr. Iktisat had given Mr. Phillips. Mr. Phillips immediately went to Mr. Iktisat and asked what had happened. Mr. Iktisat said he had given Mr. Baba the same opinion he had given Mr. Phillips. Then Mr. Baba had asked what procedure would be followed if a limited dividend were voted, and the paper was his response to that hypothetical question. The two of them then went to Mr. Baba and asked him to explain his position. Mr. Baba said that Mr. Phillips had misunderstood him and that he had said, "If! If Wadi were to declare a dividend, Mr. Iktisat suggested one of $30,000." There was no further discussion of a dividend.

Early in the following year, plans for a new factory evolved. The government was pressing for production of more drugs. The other two firms were planning new factories whose modern, clean appearance would give them a competitive lift. A team of Canton technical experts advised that new equipment would cut costs. Plans were made for a new plant capable of producing 25 percent more output at 20 percent lower labor costs per unit of output. The plant would cost $1,000,000 of which $100,000 would be recovered from sale of the existing facilities.

There was some reluctance among the Zardinian members of the board over this major investment, but on the whole they accepted it as sound. There was substantial disagreement over the method of financing. Mr. Baba proposed that the bulk of the money be raised by issuing new stock which he felt could be sold at a premium of 400 percent; i.e., whereas the founders paid $40 per share, the new issue would be sold at $200 per share. He felt he could sell the shares to the oil-rich emirs and sheiks of the Persian Gulf. To attract these buyers, he proposed that an interim dividend of 50 percent of the original capital be issued.

Mr. Phillips believed Wadi should retain its full earnings then estimated at about $200,000 for use in the new investment. He felt that investors would look more to the company's earnings than to its dividends and that a large dividend might actually discourage them. He also felt that a much smaller premium in the stock price was all that could be expected.

This case involves some interesting operational questions, but its relevance in the context of this chapter lies in the interaction of American ways with two aspects of the host society: the political-business system and interpersonal relations.

Analysis of the political-business system suggests that a significant change may be imminent in which the U.S. company may play a constructive role. Figure 3.5 shows the main elements of the established system and of the new one which may be emerging. The prevailing norm shown at the top is dominated by politico-

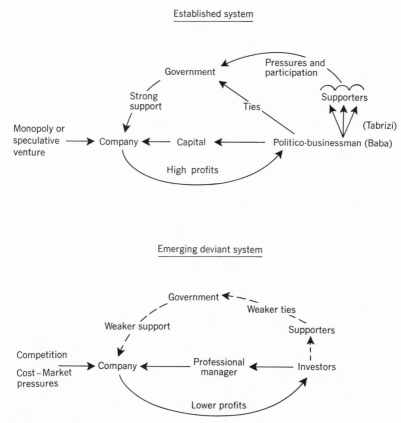

Figure 3.5 Canton Drug Company case: Zardinian political-business system.

businessmen like Mr. Baba. They provide the initiative and capital for business ventures. The success of the ventures stems in large part from their influence in government circles which results in various forms of support for their enterprises. With this support the ventures are able to generate substantial profits which are fed through the political system to assure the continuation of support. In its initial stages the Wadi Drug Company fitted this pattern. Mr. Baba demonstrated his influence in getting the production license promptly to the exclusion of most competitors. The company made a handsome profit of about 80 percent on initial capital in its first full year, suggesting that prices and other factors were adjusted very favorably. And virtually all earnings were being drained off into the supporting system immediately. This pattern has clearly been effective and must, therefore, be regarded as functional and a satisfactory norm for the moment.

Now, however, a deviation from this norm is taking shape along the lines shown at the bottom of Figure 3.5. The dominant elements of this system are market competition and the professional manager. The competition does two things. First, it greatly reduces profit margins, destroying the incentives for the politician-investor and the resources which he could use to obtain support in government circles. Second, it puts a premium on efficient management and thus enhances the position of those with managerial skills. Analysis of projected operating data shows that the Wadi profit would be about 20 percent of capital in light of the large investment for the new factory required to meet the competition of the other firms. Mr. Baba being a pretty shrewd man, it is a fair guess that he has figured out these results. Thus his scheme to pay out a large dividend and obtain the capital from new investors looks like a move to withdraw the maximum possible money and extract himself so far as possible from a situation which is no longer suitable for his *modus operandi*. Mr. Phillips on the other hand is responding to the situation in a manner consistent with the logics of the emerging system which is moving essentially in the direction of U.S. business norms.

One can expand in detail along these lines but our immediate purpose has been served by observing the basic contrasts of these two systems. The first has been the norm throughout most of the Middle East over the recent past. It is functional in a society at a low stage of industrial development dominated by the merchant's speculative psychology and unstable politics. With increasing industrialization and the development of more stable, responsible government, one can see functional utility in the second system, and the Wadi case clearly demonstrates that it is emerging.

Without a broad study of the Zardinian situation, it is, of course, impossible to determine the degree to which each of these systems prevails. It is a fair guess that the first is still the norm and that the second is as yet just a significant deviant. If this is so, then Canton has a difficult problem in deciding how to handle the conformity-innovation issue. Over the long term, innovation seems in order so as to participate fully in the achievements of those who work with the emerging system. That is, the company should be adjusting the operations of Wadi so that it has managerial effectiveness to meet the new competition aggressively. One may speculate, for example, that it would be harmful to this objective to bring into the structure a group of oil-rich Arabs who will be money-hungry and unsophisticated in management. On the other hand, over the short run, if the politico-businessman system remains the norm, the support of Mr. Baba can be of great value. So the optimum strategy for the company would seem to be some plan which will provide Mr. Baba with a continuing flow of good profits but with Canton relatively free to control the operations of Wadi.

The question of interpersonal relations is not so complex, but it does provide a striking case of cultural difference and the hazards of an American trying to deal with a foreigner by American ways. Mr. Baba is a product of merchant society, a system of relatively small enterprises each of which deals with others on an arm's-length basis with discontinuity possible at any time with no great loss of effectiveness. In such a society the merchant is essentially a lone wolf, keeping most of his thoughts to himself, bargaining and maneuvering in relations with others according to what seems best for his immediate purposes. Mr. Phillips, on the other hand, is a product of the U.S. big-company, industrial society in which the manager has wide-ranging contacts both within his company and outside it in which continuity and mutual trust are of great value. He has been conditioned to put a high value on teamwork, the exchange of information, and the generation of trust in others. One could elaborate on these characterizations and their cultural origins, but it will suffice here to note the main lines of contrast.

The contrast appears clearly in the exchange centering around Mr. Iktisat. Mr. Baba was, it appears, doing some tricky maneuvering to get his own way about the dividend. By his standards the obvious deceit was subject to criticism only to the extent that it failed, not that it was wrong. Mr. Phillips, it seems, has to a degree adjusted his ways to conform to the norms of Mr. Baba's society. The fact that he did not immediately disclose to Mr. Baba that he had the written statement from Mr. Iktisat suggests that. But one wonders if he is really doing an effective job of conforming or whether he is somehow trying to innovate by pressure on Baba. Because of the importance of Mr. Baba in Canton's operations, it scarcely seemed useful to confront Mr. Baba with the statement at a later stage so that he was embarrassed.

Again we do not really know enough to reach any clear conclusions, but the contrast in the people and the situations which evolve from the contrast illustrate the conformity-innovation problem at the personal level. As the overall norms change along the lines suggested above, from the political-business system to the managerial system, the norms of personal attitudes and behavior in business will also change. The role of external businessmen like Mr. Phillips in this process is likely overall to be positive: by example, by teaching, and so forth. But it will vary from case to case. Sometimes, it will be quite effective, for example, when the foreigner works with a young, flexible management recruit. In others, however, it may be unproductive or even counterproductive if the local national is incapable of change. This is probably true in the relations between Mr. Phillips and Mr. Baba. Thus, if the former is in fact trying to change Mr. Baba's ways of thinking and acting by his own combination of U.S. and Middle Eastern behavior patterns, he is probably wasting his time.

SUMMARY

These four situations have only been sketched in broad outline. The reader may wish to fill out in greater detail the business activities involved and the environmental factors affecting them. The sketched outlines, however, are sufficient to validate the conceptual framework proposed in this chapter. In each situation we have seen that the norms of business were tied in with the prevailing structure of economic and personal relationships, but that deviants from these were feasible if they were functionally effective. Their effectiveness stemmed essentially from changes in the host society for which the old norms were no longer a fully satisfactory response.

All these confirm the basic conceptual guidelines developed in the chapter. The roles of the multinational firm as a transmitter of resources and as a cross-cultural change agent inherently favor efforts toward innovation in the host society. The critical limiting factor in determination of strategy is the feasibility of accomplishing innovations. In this determination the main criterion is the usefulness of the innovation in the evolving pattern of the host society. A strategy of introduction of functionally effective innovations should be successful. For aspects of operations in which innovation appears dysfunctional, conformity is a sound strategy to maximize the acceptability of the firm in the host systems. These concepts are broadly sufficient with respect to the internal structure of the host society. Further strategy considerations must be developed in the next chapter to encompass the particular responses in the host society to the multinational firm as a foreign body.

Chapter Four
Conflicts with Nationalism
and National Interests

The transmission of resources and the introduction of changes in host societies provide the creative logic for the activities of the multinational firm. The analysis in the previous two chapters has focused on benefits from these processes for both the multinational firm and the host societies. But our conceptual framework will not be complete without dealing also with the conflicts which have already intruded into the previous chapters and which appear to be inherent in the processes.

To define the nature of these conflicts, we will return to the definition of international business given in Chapter 1—namely, that it encompasses business processes intersected by national borders. We have on one side of a border a firm which is part of a nation-state, and on the other side of the border another nation-state within which the firm has certain business relations. In our modern society the nation-state has become the major focal point for an assortment of attitudes and goals of people which we broadly term *nationalism* and *national interests*. The evidence of history is such that there is no need to defend the assertion that the nationalism and national interests of nations often conflict with each other and further that the conflicts are often economic in nature. The word "conflict" may imply sharp political cleavages and even war, but the intended meaning here is much broader. It encompasses all situations in which the ends sought by two nations are mutually exclusive whether it be a major issue like the desire of one to seize part of the territory of another or a smaller one like the exclusion by one nation of certain types of managers who are citizens of another. The basic source of the conflicts encountered in cross-border business processes lies in the fact that the multinational firm is caught between and is an active participant in the conflicts between the nationalism and national interests of the countries with which it has business relations.

The objective in this chapter, therefore, is to develop an analytical approach to identifying the character of the conflicts of nationalism and national interests affecting the multinational firm and to determining the lines along which the conflicts are resolved.

Although nationalism and national interests each compose a major and distinguishable subject, they are treated together here because they are so intimately intertwined in their impact on the multinational firm. It is helpful to understand the separate character of each, but in policy formulation they must frequently be considered a composite feature of the political environment. Thus in this chapter we will look first at the nature of each and its relation to overseas business and then consider the conceptual approach of management to them as a whole.[1]

NATIONALISM

Nationalism is a nebulous, complex thing which is not readily defined. Louis Snyder provides the following as a workable definition.

> Nationalism is a condition of mind, feeling, or sentiment of a group of people living in a well defined geographic area, speaking a common language, possessing a literature in which the aspirations of the nation have been expressed, being attached to common traditions, and, in some cases, having a common religion.[2]

He immediately notes, however, that "there are exceptions to every part of this definition and goes on to quote observations by others which indicate dynamic aspects of nationalism which are quite relevant here: Hahn Kohn—"the individual's identification of himself with the 'we-group' to which he gives supreme loyalty"; Carl-

[1] Substantial portions of this chapter are adapted by permission from Fayerweather, "19th Century Idealism vs. 20th Century Realism," *Columbia Journal of World Business,* Winter, 1966, pp. 77–84.

[2] Louis L. Snyder (ed.), *The Dynamics of Nationalism,* D. Van Nostrand Company, Inc., Princeton, N.J., 1964, p. 2.

ton J. H. Hayes—"a fusion of patriotism with a consciousness of nationality"; and Boyd C. Shafer—"Everywhere men seek realization of their dearest dreams . . . within their nations. Everywhere they erect their nations into bulwarks, no matter how weak, against adversity. This devotion to their nation we call nationalism."

Although nationalism is relatively new, its psychological roots are not. Nationalism is a manifestation of a fundamental human trait. The key motivation at work is the quest of man for security, reinforced by other social satisfactions which come from participation in a group. From earliest times these feelings have brought people together into groups with a high degree of internal cohesion and sharp separation from external elements. Social scientists use the term *we-group* which aptly describes the attitudes of the participants. They feel a strong identification with the group, thinking of it and acting in it on a "we" basis, and those who are not in the group are a distinctly different category: "they," "outsiders," "foreigners." The individual is raised in the traditions, culture, and values of the we-group. He is expected to and generally does willingly accept them and give them strong emotional loyalty and support. Doing so contributes greatly to his own security, for he gains both emotional and physical support from the sense that his group is good and right and strong.

For centuries these feelings found their main expression in groups which lived in relatively close physical proximity—the family, the clan, the tribe, the village, and even the city-state. These were units in which the individual could effectively share in a common life through direct interaction with other members and have a sense of participation in the group. There were large government units to be sure, but they could not serve the functions of a we-group. The great empires of Ghengis Khan and the Romans were administrative systems run by a central dictator. Early "nations" like England were affiliations of feudal rulers. Patriotism toward one's country and its monarch existed. A citizen might admire, respect, and love his king and feel emotional ties to his country. But nationalism goes a good deal beyond patriotism. The mass of the people were too poorly educated to have much knowledge of or sense of unity with "countrymen" beyond their immediate community, and they had too little participation in the government to feel full identification with it.

But there was nothing in the psychological forces involved which inherently limited we-group attitudes to small units, and two important changes, reinforced by other developments, brought forth true nationalism around the end of the eighteenth century: mass education and popular government. As literacy became quite common, facilitated by the accomplishments of the printing press, people became better acquainted with the world around them and found in this knowledge an identification with the language, traditions, literature, culture, and often religion of their national group as distinguished from the foreignness of other peoples. Concurrently the rise of the middle class was being fostered by economic growth and by the new social structure associated with the industrial revolution and large-scale manufacturing. The middle class now had a strong interest in the functioning of the national government and capacity to participate in it which superseded that of the feudal landowning aristocracy.

These limited observations, of course, gloss over a quite long and difficult transition. But in broad outline we can see how and why the we-group psychology was elevated to the national level. From its middle-class base in Europe and North America, nationalism has now spread in the company of popular government, mass communications, and independence movements to every part of the globe and down deep into the ranks of the lower classes, leaving only the most primitive tribal groups outside its range. It is found in varying stages of development, ranging from the mature forms common in Europe to the early, unstable forms in many new African nations. But everywhere it is present with most members of each nation-state now able to comprehend their affiliation with their countrymen and emotionally caught up in the sentimental affiliation to their nation-state.

For our purposes, two main characteristics of nationalism are critical. First, it is a state of mind dominant among a national population which may be likened to religion in the strength of the feelings it generates and the eminence to which it elevates national goals, traditions, and values. Second, it is almost always characterized by irrational feelings of internal loyalty and of aversion to things external to the national group.

The inherent conflict between nationalism and the multinational corporation is readily apparent. The activities of the latter are, at least to some degree, internation, either in the flow of products or the movement of capital or in some other way. Following the accepted principles of successful management, the corporation attempts to exercise from some central point at least a degree of control over activities which extend into several countries. Thus it is by definition an "outsider," something to be distrusted and repelled. Furthermore, it is an aggressive outsider seeking to enter and control a portion of life within the national group.

This inherent conflict manifests itself in a wide range of specific situations. It injects into business affairs a nonrational, adverse state of mind which most typically results in magnification of conflicts arising from rational disagreements, such as the divergence of company activities and national interests, which will be discussed in the next section. For example, the question of allocation of foreign exchange for profit repatriation for a multinational firm is frequently magnified by politicians and the press and ultimately in the minds of the populace by nationalistic reactions. Thus it becomes more of an emotional issue dominated by images of the outsider preying on the property of the we-group than a question which can be thought out fairly logically in terms of economic benefits and obligations. By the same token, within a local subsidiary, the employment of an expatriate to fill a management position will quite logically be viewed unfavorably by one or more local nationals who had aspired to the position just as would be true if no national differences were involved. But the action will frequently arouse far stronger sentiments both in the individuals immediately affected and many of their countrymen in the organization because it appears as an affront to nationalistic sentiments. It is difficult, and probably fruitless, to try to determine just how much of the conflict in a given situation arises from rational differences and how much from nationalistic reactions. The only essential point for the multinational firm to recognize is that nationalism is there and that it is dealing with something deep-seated and intangible which cannot be dispelled by logical arguments.

Though the present strength of nationalism is unquestionable, it is appropriate to ask whether this may not be a passing phase or whether nationalism has seen its peak and will be of progressively less significance to international business. The historical review presented above has two implications along this line. First, there is no reason to expect that nationalism will disappear because it is the product of immaturity or for some similar reason. The underlying we-group psychology is basic and will not disappear. Second, the past changes in the manifestations of this psychology and the reasons for the changes suggest that if new factors of the environment are favorable, new manifestations may appear.

Following the lines of historical evolution, one's instinct is to look for signs that we are moving toward a still broader span of we-group structure—the family, the tribe, the city, the nation, next perhaps an international cohesion. And indeed there are numerous things we can point to which seem to fit the requirements for such a transition. Mass communications media are making people all around the world aware of each other and familiar with each other's ways of life. There has been a steady growth of what might be called international subcultures. Teenagers, for example, in virtually all countries share tastes in hair styles, music, and the like. To at least a limited degree they show a mutual identification rising above national affiliation. The numbers involved are smaller, but we have similar trends among international businessmen, chess players, radio hams, and assorted others.

The increasing integration of the world economy is also an encouraging sign. Just as the emergence of nationalism coincided with and apparently was related to the economic suitability of the nation-state as the industrial revolution got under way, our modern economy seems to require a cohesion and cooperation among nations. The International Monetary Fund, multilateral trade agreements now centering around the GATT, and similar mechanisms rising above national sovereignties are critical to world trade and thus to the welfare of people in all nations.

But despite these favorable elements, one has to note some reasons for doubting that we are on the threshold of a true international "we-groupism." First, if we look at the past, we find that no we-group has ever existed without a "they." That is, there has always been an external world from which the we-group could distinguish itself. Whether this is cause and effect or just coincidence is impossible to determine with certainty, but the arguments for the former are certainly strong. The need for security is generally accepted as a critical motivation in the individual's commitment to the we-group. While a person may need security in relation to the unknown or in isolation, his concern about tangible external threats is strong, and its absence removes a significant support of any we-group. For international subcultures there are "theys." Teenagers everywhere, for example, are unified by their separation from adults. But a "they" distinguishable from the peoples of the world as a whole is hard to identify. The communist threat has created a degree of cohesion in the free world. But its potentials are sharply limited by the affiliation of large portions of the populations of many countries to communism. We do have a threat of sorts in the universal dread of nuclear war. Such cohesion as exists about the United Nations is due in considerable part to this fear. Yet it is hard to visualize such a nebulous threat providing bonds of the depth and variety required for a strong international we-group structure. Thus drawing the peoples of the world together tightly would seem possible only if some concrete "they" appears like a threat from outer space.

Likewise, for all the development of international subcultures, the differences among the nations are still very great and in important respects show little sign of diminishing appreciably. In such vital respects as language, religion, and cultural values the Indian, the Japanese, the German, and the American are still a very long way apart. One cannot, therefore, readily conceive of their developing a strong sense of mutual identification such as characterizes a we-group.

A look at the South in the United States and at Europe may provide useful indications of the direction in which these conflicting forces may lead. Southerners have been assimilated into U.S. nationalism, but they seceded once and at times have appeared on the verge of doing so again. The typical individual in the Deep South today may have a stronger we-group affiliation to the South than to the people of the United States as a whole. Despite a tremendous body of common language, culture, etc., with other Americans, the powerful forces are the common tradition and ways of life of the South *and* the external threat from the other Americans trying to change that way of life.

In Europe, on the other hand, it is just possible that we are seeing a true breakthrough from a national to a regional we-group structure. Although there are a multitude of differences among the countries, it is hard to identify any major deviations of political and social ideology such as separate the South from the rest of the United States. A strong base for a community of interest has been laid economically, and there is a considerable common tradition, especially in the hardship of two major wars. The fact that much of the fighting has been internal is not apparently a block, for most of our nations are composed of people who have at one time or another engaged in bitter internal fights. And, finally, between the United States and Russia, the Europeans have an ample supply of "theys" as foils for strong we-groupism.

This analysis is clearly not definitive. It suggests some reason to hope that the we-group instincts of people may be shifting from nationalism toward a broader base, especially toward regional affiliations; however, it also indicates that the prospects for major or rapid change are not encouraging. In the determination of management policies this conclusion is significant because some people have suggested that the hope for the future of international business lies in the creation of a *supranational* corporation. Ideally it would be chartered by the United Nations, have its headquarters in some center with minimal national character (like Luxembourg), be owned by stockholders of a broad range of nationalities, and be managed as a true world enterprise without partiality to any country.

Although this is an appealing idea, it will not be an effective response to nationalism unless the peoples of the world start to transfer their we-group emotions to the United Nations in substantial measure. It is effective in reducing the impact of nationalism of the home country of the multinational corporation, but it does not alter the basic relationship with other countries. The supranational corporation is still an outsider, still a "they" whether it be of United States origin or United Nations origin. Furthermore, the change would amount in large part to a fiction if, as seems likely, the capital and management of the corporation still come from a small number of major industrial countries. It might even have a negative effect because, despite all their adverse comments about capital from particular countries, especially the United States, many foreign nations may have considerably more confidence in the beneficence and responsibility of business based in a major industrial nation than in the qualities of a floating corporation chartered by a very weak world-government institution and presumably virtually free of overall government control. This is not to say that the concept may not, in fact, prove sound but only to emphasize that at the moment it is unduly favored by the age-old advantages of "the grass in the next pasture."

There is another way to look at the role of nationalism which we should consider—namely, the degree to which it is an effective force in different phases of life. In some phases like pure scientific research, nationalism is of much less importance than others like political affairs. Regrettably business has been one in which nationalism has played a prominent role because of the heavy influence which external business has exerted on the internal social and political affairs of many nations, especially the less developed ones. Animosity toward foreign investment is therefore part of the nationalistic tradition which binds these people together. Thus we start at a tremendous handicap in proposing that multinational business affairs become disassociated from nationalism.

On the other hand, it is hard to escape the historical indications that government policies have always tended to support the basic economic and business system which was desirable for the effective use of the technology of the day. If the multinational corporation is in fact beneficial economically, there is a supposition here that government policies and the national sentiments behind them will in some way be adjusted to accommodate them. In speculating about ways in which this might happen, another feature of past history is worth observing. Throughout the prenationalism eras, various forms of internationalism existed. There were administrative unifications like the Roman and Ottoman empires in which locally recruited bureaucracies served, what was for those times, quite international systems, despite the gulf between their masters and the local we-groups to whom they had an initial loyalty. Likewise, in the Renaissance period in Europe, the elite intelligentsia of the whole area were in a sense a distinctive we-group unto themselves apart from the masses. They spurned localism in favor of a common mission in a unified Catholic society. Most spoke French rather than the tongue of their country, and they disdained association with petty local interests.

The evolution of international subcultures mentioned above fits this concept. At least with respect to matters central to their bond of affiliation, the members of these groups do seem for the most part to rise above nationalism. A geographically more limited but still essentially similar grouping is found in the *third-culture* concept.[3] The third culture is composed of that group of local nationals and foreigners in a country who provide the bridge between the host society and activities originating in foreign cultures including foreign business, government (notably foreign aid programs), and educational and religious operations. The distinctive characteristic of these people is their capacity to work effectively with people from a different culture and as a corollary the weakening of their emotional ties to their own culture. Although the anthropologists who have developed this concept have emphasized the cultural aspect, it is clear that the operational logics and personal associations involved provide a comparable basis for weakening of nationalistic ties.

There would seem, therefore, to be at least some hope that localized third-culture groups or an international subculture composed of international businessmen and the government officials who work with them around the globe may achieve such a sense of unity and disassociation from internal nationalism. The prospects along this line are intriguing, and we shall return to them later in the chapter when management policies are examined. A key question in that discussion will be the extent to which a true community of interests exists, drawing managers of the multinational firm and officials of the host nation together. This element leads naturally therefore into consideration of national interests.

NATIONAL INTERESTS

Moving from nationalism to national interests, we shift from a vague, nebulous subject to one in which the problems are quite specific and tangible. We are dealing here with concrete national goals and endeavors which relate in some way to the activities of the multinational firm. The subject is a broad one, encompassing interests of the country in which the firm is based as well as those of other countries in which it functions and the interests of individuals and groups within these nations as well as the interests of

[3] John Useem, John D. Donoghue, and Ruth H. Useem, "Men in the Middle of the Third Culture," *Human Organization*, Fall, 1963, pp. 169–179.

each nation as a whole. Indeed it would appear that practically every action of the firm which touches its environment involves some aspects of national interests.

To develop this subject as a part of our conceptual framework, we may start with the transmission of resources between countries discussed in Chapter 2. A pattern of benefits, conflicts, and controls arises in this process whose key components are depicted in Figure 4.1. Country A, within which the multinational firm is based, has certain resources which offer sufficient internal benefit for country B to justify payments to country A. Thus in broad terms there is a mutually beneficial basis for economic interchange between the two nations, and national interest calls for execution of the interchange so that A may make good use of its resources and B receive benefits which are economically desirable for it. The multinational firm is the agent through which the process of interchange is accomplished. Thus many of the problems it encounters are in essence those of the nation-to-nation interchange process.

Although the interchange process is properly assumed to be mutually beneficial (otherwise it would not normally take place), its execution almost inevitably involves some degree of conflict both

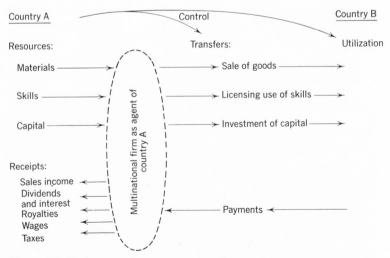

Figure 4.1 Nation-to-nation resource transfers.

as to economic terms and control. The economic terms determine in effect the division of the benefits among the participants. Country A in our example naturally seeks the maximum return for the resources employed abroad, while country B wishes to hold to a minimum the price it must pay. Likewise, country A, wishing to assure that its resources are used in the manner most profitable to it and adequately protected so long as it retains an interest in them, seeks to exercise certain controls over them. Country B, in receiving the resources, desires to exert its control to assure that they effectively serve its national interests. The multinational firm as the vehicle through which the exchange process is taking place becomes the active agent on behalf of country A in bargaining for the economic terms and establishing controls.

The problems for the multinational firm stem both from the inherent conflict between the two nations and from differences between the way the firm may see the situation and the viewpoint of the governments which serve as the overall protectors of the interests of their nations. These differences arise from divergences in opinions as to what is in the best national interest and from the difference in the terms of reference of the firm as compared with the nation as a whole. Without presuming to exhaust the many facets of this subject, we will find it useful to amplify the basic conceptual framework by citing a few of the key problems observed in international business.

First, to illustrate the *parent-nation* (country A) side of the situation, we can look at the balance of payments and tax questions encountered by U.S. multinational firms in relations with their government. Faced with persistent balance-of-payment deficits, the U.S. government arrived at the conclusion in the early 1960s that some limitation on the outflow of capital resources was in the best national interest as a means to protect the financial strength of the country. Many people, including much of the international business community, argued against this conclusion, believing that other measures would achieve the objective better. But ultimately the government view led to the voluntary restraint program instituted in 1965, followed by mandatory restrictions in 1968 which resulted in U.S. firms holding their export of capital below the level they would have set if their own judgment had been followed. In this case, the government view of the nation-to-nation exchange process was that the overall interest of the United States was best served by a limitation of resource transfer, and the U.S. firms as the agents in the process acted accordingly despite opposing views among some of them.

The major tax development was the extension of U.S. taxation to cover the retained earnings of certain types of overseas subsidiaries of U.S. firms in 1962. Previously it had been an established policy that overseas earnings of subsidiaries would not be taxed until they were actually received in the form of dividends by the parent firm. However, the U.S. government had become concerned over the way many firms were retaining most of their earnings in *tax-haven companies* in Switzerland, Panama, and certain other countries from which they were used for further investments. The effect of this process was to preclude the U.S. government from taxing away any share of the profits for extended periods. The issue was widely debated in terms of legal principles, practical business requirements, and economics with a fair amount of political byplay in the background which cannot be covered here.[4] Suffice for our purposes to observe that a critical element was the feeling in Washington that the United States was not getting an adequate return from the U.S. capital employed overseas, that in this instance the multinational firms as its agents were keeping too much to themselves and that the public was entitled to a greater share of the benefits. This view eventually prevailed in Congress, and the 1962 Revenue Act extended U.S. taxation to cover certain types of overseas retained earnings including those of the tax-haven companies.

Turning now to relations with *the host nation* (country B), we find a different range of problems. This is the point at which the terms of the nation-to-nation exchange of resources are worked out between the multinational firm as the agent for country A and the government and/or businessmen representing country B. The relatively wealthy industrialized countries are inclined to feel that their national interests will be best served by allowing these terms to be determined naturally through the free functioning of economic relations in the private enterprise system. But among the less devel-

[4] For a fuller discussion, see John Fayerweather, *Facts and Fallacies of International Business,* Holt, Rinehart and Winston, Inc., New York, 1962, pp. 50—64.

oped countries which are preoccupied with the problems of using limited resources to maximum advantage, it is common for the government to enter actively into the process of establishing both the economic and control terms.

The *economic terms* cover the full range of business arrangements which affect the profitability of the transfer of resources— prices, credit terms, and so on. In large part their negotiation is no different from similar processes in domestic business. The chief distinction is the critical role of governments, especially in the less developed countries, in such issues as price controls and taxes which will influence profits and foreign-exchange controls and exchange rates which will determine the amount of income which can be transferred back to country A. The multinational firm commonly finds itself either confronted with established policies (e.g., country B will allow repatriation of profits only up to 8 percent of capital per year) or flexible situations in which it can negotiate with the government (e.g., country B will exempt a new investment from taxation for five years if the company can argue effectively that it fills an essential national need). The firm, of course, pursues its negotiations and decision making essentially on the basis of its private interests (though the effect of such measures as the U.S. government investment guarantees is to inject some extra weighting of the parent-government's view of national interest.) In the process, however, it fulfills the role of agent for its country, establishing the terms of the nation-to-nation exchange. Whether the economic terms are determined in relations with private enterprise or the government of country B, the difference in the national interests of the two countries, each seeking to maximize its net benefits from the exchange, makes a degree of conflict inevitable.

The questions concerning *control* are not so readily defined as those relating to the division of economic benefits. They are of frequent concern, however, not only because of the national interests involved but also because the extent of controls exercised by the multinational firm within a host country has much to do with the extent to which nationalistic antagonism is directed toward it. One can set forth two extreme viewpoints: (1) that country A and the multinational firm as its agent would like to have complete control over all aspects of the use of its resources in country B and (2) that country B would like to see the resources turned over completely to its nationals as soon as they enter the country. However, neither extreme is a very close approximation of the positions found in reality. Typically, country A viewpoint accepts as beneficial to its own national interest substantial control by people in country B who are assumed to be competent to make more effective use of the resources in some respects than country A nationals could achieve, and country B position sees merit in some degree of active participation of the multinational firm in the control of the resources in its country. The problems therefore lie in a limited band of disagreement representative of (1) situations in which the national interests of the two countries diverge and (2) situations in which the multinational firm disagrees with country B as to how the national interests of that country will be best served.

The clearest example of the first category, the difference in national interests, is the question of property protection. If capital resources of country A are transferred to country B but with ownership retained by one of its companies, country A has an obvious national interest in protecting them. Although such extremes are rare today, in the not too distant past this interest was periodically manifested by active military intervention in foreign countries by nations which saw the property of their citizens threatened. Country B, on the other hand, has no great worry on this count. Typically responsible host governments are concerned with the problem to some degree because they know that they cannot attract investments unless they have a reputation for giving them reasonable protection. But this is a much less forceful concern than that of the actual owner of the capital resources. Thus capital-exporting nations and their businessmen are usually very anxious to negotiate controls to protect their property, whereas the recipient countries are reluctant to agree as the terms involved usually restrict them in ways which may impair other efforts to further national interests such as their freedom to allocate foreign exchange to other uses than capital repatriation.

The situations in the second category are by definition of a hazier nature because they are matters in which there are differences of opinion regarding how to accomplish the same goal—the advancement of the interests of the host nation. There is natural disposition along the lines discussed in Chapter 2 for the multinational firm to feel that its resources will be utilized most effectively if it exercises a substantial degree of control over the process. The better utilization is seen as beneficial both to the firm and to the country. This position is supported by the intensive study of foreign firms in Brazil by McMillan, Gonzales, and Erickson, which concluded that the general effect of national restrictions and sentiments was to prevent the foreign firms from making their full potential contribution to Brazilian economic development. It is difficult to reach any sure determination on such matters, however, because much depends on how one defines "effective utilization of the resources." For example, on the employment of local national managers, they observe "that general criticism of the prevalent practice of staffing top management positions with U.S. citizens is difficult to justify. The most significant import for the developing nation is the economic decision maker and initiator. The more and the better the quality of this class, the more rapid the pace of growth and the greater the opportunity for the development of national economic leadership." [5] In the immediate sense of the effectiveness of specific company decisions, their conclusion seems well grounded. However, the host government may be more concerned with the development of managerial skills and the amenability of companies to acceptance of government guidance, feeling that both of these are more beneficial to the overall, long-term utilization of the resources brought in by foreign firms. Those criteria lead toward maximum use of local nationals even if there is a short-term lowering of the quality of decision making in their firms. This type of difference in basic frame of reference can be found behind divergences in opinion about control of other aspects of the flow of resources such as marketing, technology, and finance.

Host nations generally feel that their national interests are best served if foreign firms have a minimum of control over the flow of goods within their economies. They reason that wholesaling and retailing are activities which their nationals are quite capable of performing and that the benefits of employment and profits from these functions should be reserved fully for their country. They also resist for nationalistic and often practical reasons the indirect

[5] Claude McMillan, Jr., Richard F. Gonzales, and Leo G. Erickson, *International Enterprise in a Developing Economy*, The Michigan State University Press, East Lansing, Mich., 1964, p. 223.

influences which the firms exert on the distribution process, especially through advertising. Foreign-style advertising is seen as perverting the national culture, and it can be directed at goals which are counter to conceived national interests (e.g., promotion of luxury products in a poor country seeking to concentrate on basic industrial development).

The foreign firm, on the other hand, will often seek to exert substantial influence on the distribution process. In doing so, it is motivated primarily by its own interest, feeling that it can do a better job of some phases of marketing than the local nationals. But it can also argue that the very fact that it can do a more effective marketing job is a contribution to host national interests in stimulating economic development and performing economic functions more efficiently. In most less developed countries, especially among government officials, this line of reasoning is not readily accepted because marketing has been held in low esteem. But it has been receiving increasing support from many sources ranging from the respected economist Walt Rostow to Russian economic planners. So this is an area in which the multinational firm may argue with some persuasion that host-country self-interest can be served better if the firm exerts greater control.

With respect to the transfer of technology, the issue of control typically revolves around the host country advocating use of licensing arrangements with local firms rather than subsidiaries of the multinational firm. The feeling is that it should be possible for the multinational firm to provide manuals, specifications, and other written material supplemented by educational and advisory services which can convey technical and managerial skills to local nationals without the necessity for ownership control. Although experience has shown that this form of transfer is feasible, there are, as we noted in Chapter 2, many managers who are convinced that it is less effective than an integrated organization in which the control of personnel and processes is better organized and more continuous. Thus they have an arguable point in claiming that the host nation may achieve greater benefit in the transfer of skills if multinational firms exercise substantial control of the process.

The question of control of financial resources typically focuses on the extent to which capital should be channeled into existing or new local companies in which the multinational firm has a minor ownership role. Multinational firms generally prefer full or majority control. Although several factors bear on their position, one of their main contentions is that they can run the business more efficiently than a local national management. To the extent that they are right, it is possible to argue that their control serves also the host national interests, for its economy should also benefit from efficient management. This is essentially an extension of their position on the transfer of skills to cover the broader competence of decision making for an ongoing business. They observe that the capacity to utilize capital resources effectively requires specialized methods and experience which they already have but which a local firm frequently does not possess.

It is not easy to mediate between the viewpoints of the multinational firms and host governments because of the different frames of reference from which they originate. However, it is useful to go back again to the underlying logics of the role of the firm in transmission of resources, especially skills, and in innovation. Our prior analysis has already suggested that effectiveness in achievement of this role is greater where the firm can exercise greater control. Thus, in the performance of the role which is understood to be beneficial to both the firm and the host country, the stronger argument would appear to lie on the side of greater control by the firm.

An interesting confirmation of this general thesis is provided by the experience of the International Basic Economy Corporation,[6] IBEC, established by the Rockefeller family, is a profit-making company; but it is primarily oriented toward upgrading the basic economies of less developed countries. All its ventures are designed to provide critically needed technological, managerial, or entrepreneurial inputs whose prior absence is often attributable to strong cultural resistance. Thus, its operations fit well into the model of the role of the multinational firm as a transmitter of resources and innovator. At the same time, its social consciousness (along with the Rockefeller association) has made it extremely sensitive to national attitudes. If any company will bend to nationalistic sentiment, it is IBEC. It has gone to great ends to serve other countries' interests and convey a favorable image to the public. It

---

[6] Wayne G. Broehl, Jr., *The International Basic Economy Corporation*, National Planning Association, Washington, 1968.

has no strong "market-position" objectives nor a great need to remit profits home as has the typical multinational firm. Given these characteristics, the fact that IBEC holds firmly to retention of control is most significant. It has found that "investment in less developed countries *not* accompanied by management control has had a very poor record." [7]

The IBEC experience apparently confirms the conclusion that where the multinational firm is performing the role for which it is fundamentally useful in transmission of skills and innovation, the maintenance of control is sound. The complementary conclusion would also appear to follow, that is, if control does not serve a useful purpose in a given case, then it is quite possible that the multinational firm does not have a significant role to play. Clearly, generalizations from either conclusion to all cases are not practical. But the logics and experience underlying them do provide some basis for sorting out the issues under analysis in the direction of those in which control by the multinational firm is related to its basic role and those in which the issue of control may be merely a superficial symptom of weakness of the basic contributions of a firm.

Summarizing this section, we have observed that the activities of the multinational firm inevitably affect the national interests of both the parent and host countries. Although a degree of mutual benefit for both countries must underlie these activities, some degree of conflict of interests is generally present. Further complications arise because of differences in perceptions of what the true national interests are and because of the special interests of the multinational firm. The interplay of the various interests appears most in the establishment of terms of exchange and the degree of control to be exercised by the firm and the host nation in the transmission of resources.

POLICY FOR THE MULTINATIONAL CORPORATION

In the establishment of policies for the multinational corporation, two features of the nationalism—national interest complex we have been examining are fundamental: first, that there is a substantial

---

[7] *Ibid.*, p. 280.

degree of uncertainty among the various parties as to what is in the best interests of each and, second, that some degree of conflict with nationalism and national interests is inevitable. These features, in turn, suggest two levels of policy formulation for our conceptual framework. At the first level the corporation should devote its efforts to the achievement of all feasible accommodations to nationalism and national interests, seeking to minimize conflicts and to maximize the achievement of mutual benefits. At the second level, policies must be designed which recognize valid conflicts and achieve a workable dynamic balance based on relative benefits and power relationships.

The discussion which follows will be confined to policies in relations between the multinational corporation and host nations. The other side of the question—relations with the parent country—is not considered unimportant; but relatively speaking, such relations are much less difficult, and insofar as this book is concerned, it is not essential to deal with them because conceptually the approaches to them are essentially the same as with host nations. That is, in broad concept (though not of course in specific detail) the accommodation and power-balance approaches are fully applicable to relations with the parent country. Thus describing the conceptual framework for policy formulation will be adequately served by examining these approaches as applied to host-nation relations.

THE ACCOMMODATION APPROACH

The achievement of feasible accommodation between the multinational firm and a host nation is directed at the range of decision options in which differences in views are due to deficiencies of perception, inertia, or related causes rather than valid conflicts. Figure 4.2 illustrates this concept. On most questions there will be some span of difference X-Y, which represents a range of true conflict in the interests of the host nation and the multinational firm. But each party will usually conceive its interest as extending beyond these limits because of failure to understand the full situation, unwillingness to shift from an earlier position, nationalistic emotions, or some other reason. This misconceived extension of

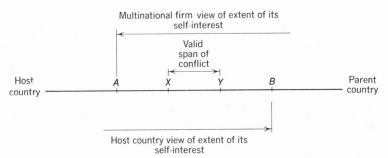

Figure 4.2 Conflicts in views of self-interest.

self-interest is represented by the added bands *A-X* and *B-Y* on either side of the span of valid conflict. Thus in many issues the parties find they are divided by an *A-B* span which is much wider than the *X-Y* span over which conflict is really justified. The distinction between the valid scope of self-interest and the misconceived range of its extensions is, of course, impossible to determine accurately in practice. Because of the varied values and goals of people within one group and the difficulty of obtaining full and objective facts and predictions of consequences of actions, one can never arrive at a clear determination as to the true interest of a group in any situation. However, the distinction is meaningful in broad terms and is useful in the conceptual framework being developed here.

The question of the use of local nationals in management jobs in subsidiaries can be used as an example. In a particular situation a multinational firm, we will assume, has sound logic in arguing that *its interests* are best served if the general manager and perhaps the senior financial officer are parent-country nationals, but the host government has equal logic in saying that *its national interests* call for using local nationals in these positions. This is the *X-Y* span of basic conflict, and its disposition will be considered later.

But on either side of this span there may well be other viewpoints. The *A-X* range indicates the views of those executives in the firm who advocate employment of expatriates in middle and perhaps even lower ranges of management, and the *B-Y* range covers host-nation views that expatriates should be excluded from even such activities within the subsidiary as staff advisors or a permanent stockholder's representative. These viewpoints are apparently not based on sound conceptions of self-interest.

The *A-X* range may be due to a biased underrating of the managerial capabilities of local nationals or the determination of expatriates presently holding jobs abroad to keep them when actually very able local nationals can be found who could do a good and perhaps better job with lower total compensation than expatriates. The *B-Y* range, on the other hand, can be traced to excessive nationalistic worry over foreign control of national industry or pressures from professional groups seeking to capture every possible job for local nationals without recognition of the real gain to the nation in some degree of facilitation of the inflow of resources by representatives of the parent company on the spot.

The problems of achieving feasible accommodation are readily apparent in this example. In the first place, it is no easy matter to determine the *X-Y* span. In practically every situation it will differ. Thus while the general manager–financial officer issue is very often the point at which valid interests collide, in other cases such as the oil companies in Saudi Arabia, employment of expatriates at much lower positions is clearly beneficial to the host nations because of the lack of competent local nationals. Likewise, in a number of cases, especially in Europe, a company can find a local national who is both highly competent and sufficiently loyal to company interests so that his employment as general manager is in its best interests. But any such conclusion is clearly based on subjective evaluation of many ill-defined variables and human characteristics. The same is true of other issues such as how much ownership should be shared with nationals, proper competitive relationships, and the like.

The underlying problem therefore is one of discernment—to determine what the *A-X* and *B-Y* spans are—and then one of implementation. For the multinational firm these are essentially human problems involving intellectual effort, emotional discipline, and personal motivations. Their character is illustrated by one conclusion coming out of the intensive research among U.S. companies conducted by Richard D. Robinson: "An inflexible policy against entering any joint ventures was nearly always a veneer covering basic distrust by United States businessmen, and possibly dislike, of non-Americans." [8] That such attitudes should be encountered among Americans is not at all surprising because they are fully consistent with the nature of nationalism as discussed earlier in this chapter. American executives are as prone to nationalistic attitudes as those of any other nation. But they, along with equally difficult deterrents in lack of intellectual perception and in personal interests, make it hard for managements to pull back from A to X, that is, to accommodate their own policies to host-nation viewpoints where there is a valid coincidence of interests.

Dealing with the B-Y span, the host-nation side, is yet harder because essentially the same human problems are involved, but the corporation can influence them only as an outsider. There is at the outset the nationalistic resistance problem, any view advanced by the outsider, the multinational corporation, being instinctively resisted as coming from a suspect and distrusted source. One of the prime objectives of the corporation must therefore be to tone down nationalistic attitudes toward it both to reduce resistance to its views and to minimize their influence as a factor in the B-Y span. It seems evident that in many cases local nationals are to a degree blinded to their own self-interest because of nationalistic emotions. For example, many people in a host country will instinctively support the full use of local nationals in management for this sort of emotional reason and will not, therefore, make a real effort to discern when the practice will or will not actually help their national economy.

In the design of a strategy to approach this problem, it is useful to think in terms of sectors of the host society as indicated schematically in Figure 4.3. The groups are plotted roughly along a curve according to the relative strength in their views of two factors: *nationalism* and "industrialism." The latter is a term coined for convenience here to include both the degree of interest of a person in industrial development and his comprehension of the realities of accomplishing it. At the outer extremes of Figure 4.3, we have the average citizen who is interested in industrial development but who has little rational understanding of its requirements and who is strongly influenced by nationalistic sentiments.

[8] Richard D. Robinson, *International Business Policy*, Holt, Rinehart and Winston, Inc., New York, 1964, p. 148.

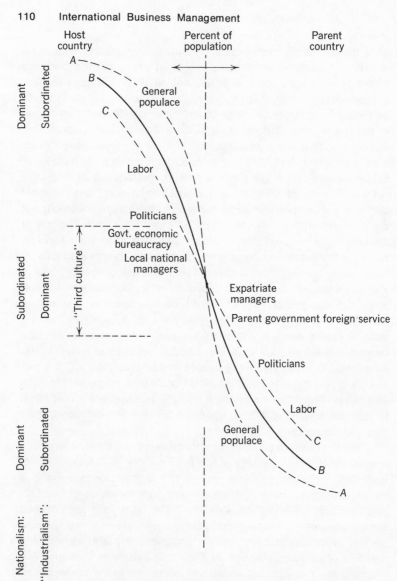

Figure 4.3 Nationalism versus industrialism (schematic diagram).

Illustrative of the attitudes toward foreign investment found at the extremities are the results of an opinion survey in Brazil which showed that two-thirds of the people felt that foreign investors should take no profits out of the country.[9] Views of this nature are characteristic of the typical "man in the street," especially in less developed countries. As a general proposition he wishes industrial development and wants foreign companies to help. But when confronted by a specific issue in which the foreign company appears to be benefiting at the expense of his country or exercising control over internal affairs, he will instinctively give a negative response arising essentially from nationalistic emotions, with little or no realistic evaluation of the merits of the issue.

As we move toward the central axis, the nationalistic views come under greater restraint with rational understanding of economic factors coming to the fore. In the center the attitudes of people on both sides of the nationality break are fairly close because in many economic considerations they are thinking alike. These people are generally members of the third culture described earlier in this chapter, including national and expatriate executives and government officials who have a substantial community of interests themselves.

Although some public relations efforts directed at the general population are doubtless worthwhile, it is not realistic to expect a notable change to be accomplished by this means. Anti-foreign investment attitudes are so deeply imbedded in the nationalistic traditions of the less developed countries and have become such prominent political footballs in even such advanced societies as France and Canada that the efforts of multinational corporations to change them can have little effect. With respect to this great sector of society therefore, the most effective strategy is likely to be to avoid public exposure of areas of conflict. For some large companies and major issues this may not be practical, but in many cases companies can in one way or another handle relations with the host government or local individuals or groups so that they do not attract public attention. This strategy then permits full attention to be directed toward people in or close to the third-culture group who have a much greater initial disposition to look upon conflicts dispassionately, emphasizing their economic and managerial content.

Two elements of strategy appear to be productive in approach-

[9] Cited in Claude McMillan, Jr., et al., *op. cit.,* p. 45.

ing the third-culture sector: first, efforts to expand the sector and, second, efforts to reduce the degree of misconceptions of valid national interest among its members, to reduce the B-Y span. In pursuit of the first element, companies find they are accelerating and facilitating a process which has already gained substantial momentum. A number of developments in recent times have been expanding the third-culture group quite rapidly, notably many international educational programs, large-scale international contacts of government personnel in aid, military, and other activities, and growing interdependence of nations. Thus we might schematically indicate the growth of the third-culture group by the shift of the line in Figure 4.3 from A-A in 1945 to B-B in the late 1960s and go on readily to visualize a C-C position as a natural evolution by 1980.

No one company can of course alter this overall progression radically, but a useful movement of people into the third culture so far as its own affairs are concerned is quite feasible. The typical company will have significant interactions with only a limited number of local nationals in business and government positions. The strategic proposition advanced here is simply that a concerted effort be made to attract these people away from strong attachment to their basic cultural and nationalistic attitudes and toward the more neutral viewpoints of the third culture. On a practical level the feasibility of this strategy has been proved by many overseas managers. The specific means of implementation are too varied to discuss here, but they generally boil down to sincere, persistent efforts to reach out to individual local nationals and draw them into the third culture by personal attraction. The success of numerous foreign executives in their business responsibilities is due in no small part to the way in which they have broadened their own immediate third-culture social orbit.

Although the reduction of emotional, nationalistic attitudes implicit in belonging to the third culture eases the task, the second element of the strategy poses real problems. There are just as many intellectual and personal blocks among host nationals as there are among managements of multinational corporations, resulting in the same inability or unwillingness to see where true national interest lies. Just to cite one striking illustration of the type of problem encountered, we may recall the expropriation of the

Iranian oil properties in 1951. Quite well-educated Iranians sincerely believed that their nationals could step right in and run the great Abadan refinery. Only bitter failure showed them that the technological complexities were beyond their capacities so that in their own national interests they found it wise ultimately to bring in a new group of Westerners to run the industry.

In a less dramatic way this sort of education by experience is constantly under way, and the essence of the second element of company strategy is to make a deliberate effort to facilitate the process. It is essentially an educational job though it may proceed in many ways. Sometimes a large-scale effort may be helpful. For example, in 1964 the Business Council for International Understanding, a group of progressively minded U.S. firms, organized a program of meetings with Indian government officials which was aimed at giving the Indians a clearer understanding of the needs and capabilities of U.S. industry and how government policies related to them.[10] More commonly the strategy calls for many and varied communications with businessmen, government bureaucrats, and other local nationals in which the facts and implications of each area of conflict are progressively discussed and understanding advanced. Again the details of the execution of such a strategy require more space than is feasible here. For one example of a well-executed effort, the reader is commended to Richard Robinson's case history of Merck's negotiations with the Indian government for establishment of a pharmaceutical plant.[11]

THE POWER-BALANCE APPROACH

Although the accommodation approach may establish a broader range of coincidence of interests, there remain inevitably the valid conflicts, the X-Y span in Figure 4.2. These valid conflicts call for a different type of policy built essentially around power relationships.

Two prefatory remarks are needed to set this discussion in per-

---

[10] *United States Policy toward Asia,* Report of the Subcommittee on the Far East and the Pacific, House Committee on Foreign Affairs, Supt. of Doc., Washington, D.C., 1966, pp. 187–207.

[11] Richard D. Robinson, *Cases in International Business,* Holt, Rinehart and Winston, Inc., New York, 1962, pp. 100–118.

spective. First, it is commonplace to observe that conflicts in human affairs are settled by power, sometimes by raw force, but more typically by the exercise of economic, legal, and political strength: workers win higher wages according to their power to withhold their productive contributions from an enterprise by striking; the price of a house emerges as a balance between the strength available to the seller (the merits of his house and often his financial staying power) and that of the buyer (chiefly his opportunity to buy alternative houses); the politician beats out his rival if he has the ability to marshal power through popular support, and so on. Thus there is nothing unusual in the observation that conflicts confronting the multinational firm must be resolved through the use of power.

The second remark takes another tack. Given the nature of nationalism, the idea that a foreign company's status in a host country is the result of the exercise of power is disturbing. There is a great temptation to sweep the whole idea under a rug and talk about "nicer" things. We have no business doing that, however. Not only is it unrealistic but, more important, it encourages a fallacious line of thinking which is all too common. There are those who propose that companies operating abroad must go all the way to satisfy the valid interests of host governments, asserting in effect that the exercise of power by the multinational firm in this context is improper. Because this position is often related to humanitarian consideration of the lower-income levels of the less developed countries and past and present shortcomings of the performance of foreign firms, it is appealing. But looking at the matter objectively, one can see no logical reason why power should not be just as normal and proper a basis for settling conflicts in the relationships of the multinational firm as in any other type of conflict.

Working from this philosophical base, we may go on to consider the elements of power present. Our analysis can be limited to economic and political power, physical force being rarely employed except as an adjunct to the former. Legal power is also not covered per se because it is essentially a consequence of economic and political power, though of course in all its ramifications it composes a very large subject quite pertinent to the effective use of power. We will look first at the power available to the multinational corporation and then at the host-nation side of the balance. In this discussion a broad distinction can often be made between the situations encountered in developed as compared to less developed countries, recognizing all the while that the problems in each country will be unique to some degree.

The power of the multinational corporation stems from the resources and political strength of the parent country which are variously distributed among the multinational corporation, other companies, and the government. This basic power is reinforced by the power of other countries with multinational companies. The forms the power takes are best described by reference to the types of situations in which they appear.

In the precommitment stage of any transfer of resources, the corporation has available the power to withhold the resources whether they be goods proposed for sale or capital funds for a new investment or technical skills for a licensing arrangement. The strength of this form of power will, of course, vary greatly depending upon the value of the resources to the host nation. This value, as Peter Gabriel has pointed out, is essentially determined in the marketplace rather than by a determination of the intrinsic productive contribution of the resources.[12] The marketplace value, in turn, is a function of the competitive strength of the corporation in relation to other companies and countries. The weakest situation is that of the exporter of a staple commodity in ample world supply —sugar for example. A firm selling such a product can do little more than sell at the price and terms prevailing on the world market as it will gain nothing by threatening not to sell unless better terms are offered. At the other extreme we have a few companies with highly developed technological skills and great competence in applying them. The Merck case mentioned earlier is a good example. While giving the company full credit for the skill with which they accommodated Indian interests, we must also note that they were negotiating from very substantial strength in their technology both relative to other Western companies and in competition with the Russians who were not considered to be as competent by the Indians. The power of the multinational firm is under-

---

[12] Peter P. Gabriel, "The Investment in the LDC: Asset with a Fixed Maturity," *Columbia Journal of World Business,* Summer, 1966, p. 114.

scored in those cases where the initiative has come from the host country—for example, when a host-country firm seeks a licensing agreement from a multinational firm because it lacks certain technical skills. In between these extremes lies a broad range in which companies have varying degrees of power, depending upon the combination of financial resources, technical skill, managerial competence, and productive capacity at their command.

Once the initial commitment to transfer resources has been made, the power to withhold them loses much of its force, though in most cases there is a degree of future flow of resources which gives some continuing power. A drug firm, for example, will be producing new technology, the future availability of which provides at all times some power for the corporation in relations with host nations.

Although the resources under its immediate control give the corporation considerable power, it benefits substantially from other forms of power. One of the major forms is the collective willingness of other corporations, both from its own country and from other nations, to transfer resources to a country arising from opinions about its *investment climate.* With many investment opportunities available to them, multinational corporations are relatively selective, and one of their prime criteria in judging new proposals is their view of the favorableness of the investment climate, especially the treatment they may expect from the government. Their conclusions on this count are very largely determined by their observation of the way in which foreign firms presently in the country have been treated, and therein lies the power available to the individual firm.

This form of power is most pertinent in the less developed countries which are anxious to attract private investment. The situation in each country is different, but we can identify a fairly common evolution. A few years ago, the nation with an inexperienced government staffed by anticapitalist, highly nationalistic people treated foreign firms already established within its borders quite harshly. Expropriations may have occurred, but more commonly there were severe regulations; foreign exchange for dividends and even for essential material imports was erratically available; and so forth. At the same time the government was hard pressed to find resources to support economic development, and there was a growing feeling that private foreign capital must play a bigger role. Unfortunately it appeared that multinational firms were not much interested. Before long, government officials began to see that there was a connection between this fact and the way they were treating the established firms, and from this learning process arose a degree of power for the latter in their continuing relations with the government. That is, the government felt some sense of restraint in actions affecting the established firms because of concern over how these actions might appear to prospective new investors.

A second source of power in the less developed countries is the economic aid provided by the wealthier countries individually and collectively through international institutions. The donors of aid have been loath to use it in an overt manner to pressure less developed countries in their relations with multinational firms, but in assorted ways the aid programs have been a source of power to the companies. The receiving countries have had some very clear signs of the potential relationship between treatment of foreign companies and contributions of aid. For example, in 1962 the U.S. Congress passed the Hickenlooper amendment which required that U.S. aid be cut off from any nation which expropriated property of U.S. companies without prompt and adequate compensation. Although the amendment itself has not been particularly effective, this and numerous other U.S. government actions have shown less developed countries that the way U.S. firms fare in their countries will be one factor determining how they fare when aid decisions are made, and so the firms have acquired a degree of power from the aid program.

In relations in the highly industrialized countries, multinational firms draw power from the presence of foreign investments in the parent country. For example, U.S. subsidiaries in France benefit from the fact that French companies have subsidiaries in the United States. Each government tends to refrain from actions in its own country which may lead to retaliation against the investments of its nationals abroad. This is a matter of mutual respect for which the power idea may seem inappropriate, but it is fundamentally part of the same concept. The chief difference between it and the forms of power discussed above is that the situation is much more stabilized and institutionalized. That is, the extent of the power has

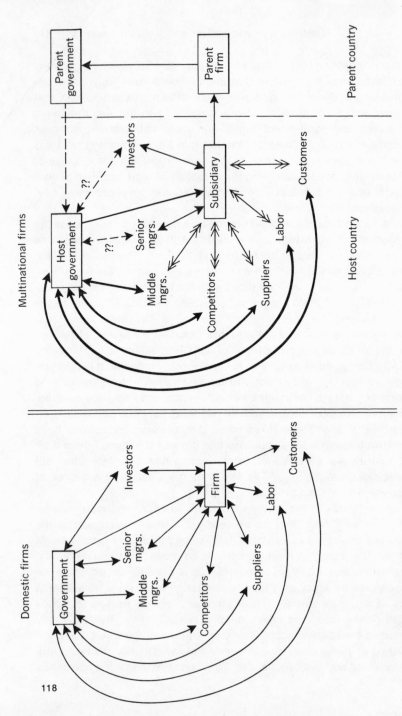

Figure 4.4 Political power relationships.

already been largely recognized for some time; and it has been given effect in treaties, routine patterns of government conduct, and other established forms which are more or less taken for granted.

The power held by the host country comes more from political relationships, though economic power is also significant. The key element in this part of the power structure is the special political status of the multinational firm which arises from its interaction with various components of the host society and the related interactions with the host government. The nature of this status and its relation to the subject of national interests can be explained by comparison of the two situations illustrated in Figure 4.4. In modern democratic nations the political system provides a means for satisfying and blending individual, group, and broad national interests.

On the left side of the figure we have a self-contained political system in which the main components interacting with the business firm are shown. Each of the interactions contains some degree of mutual benefit and some degree of conflict. For example, competitors will often collaborate in the sharing of industry statistics through an association while they battle in the marketplace. Workers earn wages by virtue of the success of a business, but they are ever anxious for a greater share of the company's income.

The resolution of the conflict aspect of the interaction is a complex matter; however, we can identify certain elements of it which are significant variables in understanding the status of the multinational firm. First, there is the sense of identity with the company which is important particularly for the groups closest to it. The clearest illustration is the expectation of future top management careers which contributes to acceptance by middle management of salary, assignment, and other conditions which, if treated on an immediate reaction basis, might lead to greater conflict. Among workers there is at least a degree of moderation of conflict due to a sense that the corporation's profits contribute to local and national development; and in some firms like Sears, Roebuck, one finds that workers own directly or through pension funds significant portions of company stock.

Second, there is the assurance that comes from knowing that each component is subject to similar conditions. Competitors, for example, have access to similar financial institutions, suppliers, and so forth. Thus they can more readily accept the character of the conflict as a fair match. This point must immediately be qualified, of course, by the observation that within a society there are all sorts of inequalities which favor one side of a conflict. With respect to competitors, for example, greater size tends to facilitate access to financial institutions. This is true, but it does not nullify the significance of the idea of similar conditions for this comparative analysis as we shall see in a moment.

The third element is equal status in voting rights and treatment by the government. A company does not, of course, have a direct vote, but through its top management and owners it is able to exercise an effective influence on the political process. The other components with which it interacts can seek recourse through the government for resolution of conflicts with the company. In some cases they may succeed. In the United States, for example, small firms have gained some relief from the disadvantages of their size through the Antitrust Act, the Small Business Administration, and other means. Sometimes they may not succeed, but the mere fact that they have recourse to the government eases somewhat the tension of conflict.

Turning now to the situation of the multinational firm in a foreign society, on the right side of Figure 4.4, we find a different story. The immediate interactions will generally have the same character as to both mutual benefits and conflicts. Middle managers, workers, competitors, and the like will have much the same degree of common interests and conflicts of interest in their regular activities with domestic firms as with a subsidiary of a multinational firm. The nature of the three elements affecting the resolution of the conflicts is, however, appreciably different with regard to the multinational firm because of its ties to the parent country and its political status in the host country.

The sense of identity of the interacting components is to some degree weakened by the flow of income back to the parent country and the control exerted by nonnationals. The workers are, therefore, somewhat less easily satisfied in their wage demands because they feel that company profits when they leave the country do not benefit them even in the small way that they might if they stayed in the host nation. Middle managers with virtually no prospect of reaching the top of the parent executive ranks and perhaps even cut off from senior subsidiary levels have less sense of identity with company goals.

By the same token, the multinational firm is seen by local national firms as operating under more advantageous conditions. It can, for example, draw on a broader range of financial resources both in its parent treasury and in access to the capital markets of other nations.

On the other hand, the political status of the multinational firm as shown in Figure 4.4 is clearly weaker. If it works through a fully owned subsidiary whose top executives are all nonnationals, it has very little political status in the normal electoral scheme. If it has a joint venture with some local stockholders and employs local nationals in senior positions, it will have some exponents with votes, but it is still weaker than a completely national firm in its direct relations with the government.

There is some compensating corrective for this weakness through the parent government, the extent of which will vary with the nature of the government and the situation in each foreign country. There were cases in the past where this factor weighed heavily for the foreign firms. For example, in China a century ago by virtue of treaty obligations imposed by their parent countries, foreign firms had extensive extraterritorial rights including being subject to their own laws, not those of China. But today, parent governments exert far less influence on foreign governments in behalf of their nationals. The U.S. government typically does not take a strong position to aid U.S. firms in their relations with foreign governments except where a pressing U.S. national interest seems to be involved. Most of its efforts are of a generalized nature in seeking, for example, nondiscriminatory treatment of investors or encouraging foreign countries to establish monetary reforms which will give greater assurance of ability to repatriate profits. The outcome of these efforts is, of course, highly dependent upon the overall relationships between the governments involved which inject into the conceptual relationship issues of broad international political affairs which are too big to discuss in this brief treatise, even though they are quite significant to it. To summarize, the support of the parent government is a factor, but it does not generally compensate for the weaker status of the multinational firm in the host-country political system so that the firm is on balance in a weaker position than local firms in this respect.

The combined effect of the differences in these three elements between the purely domestic situation and that of the multinational firm in a foreign nation is to set up a quite different flow of political forces and resultant actions as shown in Figure 4.4. The local groups interacting with the firm having less sense of identity and assurance of equal opportunity feel a greater sense of conflict in their relations with the firm. This, combined with an underlying nationalistic reaction, results in a greater flow of feelings up to the government.

The government, being a politically sensitive organ, tends to respond to these greater pressures and to the weaker ones coming from the multinational firm whose political power is limited. On the other hand, the politicians in the government often do or say things which encourage the anti-foreign investment component of nationalistic attitudes—a political stratagem which has proved effective for leaders in a great many countries. This process then tends to add to the pressures arising from the industrial relationships and creates a further component of pressure related to both nationalism and internal political byplay (e.g., the anti-foreign investment campaign oratory which must be implemented if the politician is not to be subject to opposition criticism).

The government might or might not meet fully the wishes of a particular national group or individual, depending upon other political considerations and its own view of national interest. But as often as not, there is a coincidence of national and special interests so that this political process fosters actions which in effect favor the special interests of the various groups in conflicts with the multinational firm. For example, the desire of individual local nationals to obtain high management positions fits with government concern for greater national control, so the promulgation of assorted restrictions on the use of expatriates had been facilitated. Although technically discriminatory treatment is adjured by all governments, workers can generally be sure that government labor officials will give them stronger support in negotiations with foreign firms than with local ones because of national interest in capturing as much income for the country as possible. Where special interests diverge from national interest, the outcome is unpredictable, but the weight of the political forces is likely to be significant, especially in matters such as were discussed earlier where the national interest is subject to some debate. For example, in a number of cases it would appear that joint ventures have been required by foreign governments more to satisfy the desire of local investors than to achieve optimum national economic advantage. So far as the power balance is concerned therefore, the political status of the multinational firm abroad is one of notable weakness.

The *economic power* of the host country comes from the value of the opportunity which it offers to the multinational firm and the controls which it commands. In a sale of goods this is simply a one-shot monetary payment, though there may be prospects of future sales to strengthen the buyer's hand. In investment and licensing situations the economic factor has a longer time dimension. As was noted in Chapter 2, market strategy is a prime factor in investment decisions. Multinational firms are extremely anxious to establish and maintain a strong position in foreign markets, especially the large and emerging ones. Thus host governments are well aware that they hold substantial economic power in their ability to give or withhold permission to operate in a market.

In addition, on a continuing basis the host government can control a number of factors affecting the economic performance of the firm—foreign exchange, imports, prices, and so on. In those many countries where extensive economic planning and control are exercised, it is accurate in fact to characterize the private firm as being completely at the mercy of the government. Its profitability is dependent in large measure on the decisions of bureaucrats. Whether or not decisions are made which are economically adverse to the firm will, of course, depend upon many important considerations including such countering elements of power as have already been mentioned. But that is a further question. The point being made here is simply that the government does have the capacity and facilities to take these economic measures if it wishes, and therein lies a strong element of economic power.

Another facet of this subject upon which we should reflect for a moment is the role of agreements between governments and of supranational organizations in resolution of conflicts. For the most part this role is minor, and if the earlier prediction that the shift of affiliation from the nation-state to a supranational state will be slow, it is likely to remain so. In the conceptual framework we have been developing therefore, the role appears to be one of institutionalizing the handling of certain phases of conflict resolution. That is, the agreements among nations and the supranational organizations provide a means for dealing in a collective or systematic way with conflict issues. The governments of pairs of countries have gotten together and threshed out problems of overlap in taxation. The World Bank is evolving a system of mediation of disputes involving multinational firms and host countries. In these matters and others, the primary protagonists remain the nation-states and the multinational firms. And where there is a conflict, the resolution is dependent upon the same processes of accommodation with definition of interests and ultimately of power relations. Thus the basic concept of conflict resolution is the same as that we have been considering. The added element is the facilitating intervention of the government-to-government agreement of the establishment of an institution by multigovernment agreement as in the role of the World Bank. There is every reason to assume that this sort of role will expand because it is an efficient and a systematic way to deal with situations which recur and affect many companies. Thus it is important to the strategy of the firm to know when and how to employ the devices which evolve. But this is essentially part of the execution stage of the strategy, not of the determination of the basic lines of the strategy which will remain the effort to clearly define the true interests of each party, to accommodate as far as possible to them, and to compromise the residual conflict through sound application of relative power status.

Any attempt to summarize this analysis of the power structure by drawing up a balance between the positions of the multinational corporation and the host nation is futile. The various forms of power are not susceptible to quantification, and they vary notably for each company and country situation. Thus we can only observe that there is substantial power available to each side and that the concept of policies based on a dynamic balance-of-power positions is fundamental to the formulation of corporate policies.

Before leaving the subject of power, we must add one more dimension to the picture—namely, the element of *change*. Nationalism, national interests, and the elements of power are all subject to substantial change over time. The significance of these changes for business policies is perhaps best explained by an example—that of the oil companies in the Middle East.

In the 1920s, when exploration started in the Middle East, the host countries lacked the skills and capital needed to develop a petroleum industry, so their national interests were clearly served by the resources the oil companies could bring in. Their power position was very weak because, since the presence of vast reserves of oil was as yet unknown, they were offering an opportunity of uncertain value. The seven major oil companies with still modest raw-material requirements and functioning in a restrained, oligopolistic pattern did not compete among themselves vigorously in the quest for oil reserves and thus did not contribute to the power of the host nations. All of these factors led to concession agreements which provided for modest 12.5 percent royalties for the host nations and a relatively free hand for the companies in management of the oil operations.

By the 1960s all the elements of this situation had changed notably. The host nations had now greatly increased their financial resources, and many of their nationals had acquired technical competence (though in most cases not enough to fully operate the oil industry). The existence of vast, proved reserves established the great value to oil companies of concession rights. The world demand for petroleum had mushroomed so that the companies were under constant pressure to acquire new reserves. Furthermore, instead of dealing with seven mildly competing major companies, the host countries were now receiving highly competitive offers from a variety of companies from many countries. They had still further strengthened their position by banding together with other oil-producing countries in the Organization of Petroleum Exporting Countries (OPEC) to negotiate key issues with the companies. The net effect of these basic changes was that the interests and power relationships had shifted radically in favor of the host nations. Accordingly, there had been a notable change in the terms of their relationships. Concession agreements generally were giving the host nations about 60 percent of profits and sometimes more. There were also agreements limiting significantly the management control of the companies. OPEC, for example, was exerting considerable control over pricing.

Although this situation is a rather extreme example, the types of changes involved are quite common both over the long term and in relatively short periods. Richard Robinson's penetrating historical analysis of external investments in the less developed countries points up the major long-term trends and their significance.[13] In the nineteenth century, when the investments started, the host countries were weak in economic resources, and in many cases their governmental systems were so poorly organized that they did not even have strong political power. In these circumstances, the companies providing badly needed capital and skills were powerful enough to obtain very favorable terms. With the passage of time these countries have made appreciable economic progress, and their political competence has advanced. They still have great needs for capital and skills which multinational firms can provide, but the power differential has shifted substantially in their favor.

Robinson discusses at length the difficult policy problem which this shift has caused for companies whose operations span a considerable time period. The favorable terms which were soundly established in an early period were typically formalized in some legal document, a concession agreement for example. The companies, adhering to the principles of private property rights and the enforceability of contracts, feel justified in holding the countries to these terms. The host countries, on the other hand, seeing that the balance of interests and power positions have changed say that the terms are no longer justified.

There is probably no "just" resolution to this problem. Both sides are "right" in a way. As a practical matter, however, such issues are now and will in the future be resolved on the basis of the new power positions, and the shortcomings on both sides have been more in the failure to properly assess these positions than in terms of any absolute sense of justice. The host countries have given too much weight to their growing economic and political strength, which has been supported in the public image by charges of excessive past use of power and exploitation by the Western nations and their companies. This view has led them to press harder on the multinational firms than the true power relations justify, considering their continuing needs for capital and skills, with

[13] Richard D. Robinson, *International Business Policy, op. cit.,* pp. 1–44.

the result that they have created images of poor investment climate and that their national interests have suffered. On the other hand, many established companies have held too rigidly to the legal-right position and have been overconfident of their economic strength, not recognizing the degree to which the power of the host nations has grown. This view has led to unsatisfactory relations and, in some cases, even loss of property.

The shorter-term shifts have been succinctly analyzed by Peter Gabriel:

It is characteristic of direct-investment projects that their first-order benefits are greatest, certainly most spectacular, in the initial stages of the undertaking; capital flows in, plants are built, local workers are hired and trained, local supply contracts are let. Subsequently, the benefits from the investment change in nature and become diffused. The straightforward inflow of capital is followed by export production or domestic production of goods formerly imported (import substitution). Job creation shifts from the foreign enterprise to local contractors and suppliers. The importance of new technology changes from its direct use by the foreign firm to the more subtle demonstration effects on local entrepreneurship. These benefits seldom phase out completely. Yet over time they lose much of the impact associated with the inception and initial operation of the enterprise.

The explicit *costs* of the foreign investment to the host economy generally behave in an exactly opposite fashion. They accrue almost imperceptibly at first, rise with the usual increase in the company's capital stock through plowback of earnings, and finally begin to abrade national sensitivities—in the form of dividend payouts—when the front-page benefits of the foreign investment have already sunk into oblivion, and discussion of second-, third-, and fourth-order benefits continues only in economic journals. True, remissions of earnings—though perhaps huge in comparison with the amount of capital originally brought into the country—are often modest compared with total profits realized or total capital employed. But these distinctions do not usually inform public controversy, acknowledged as they may have become in theoretical analysis.[14]

He concludes:

Now, it is characteristic of a developing country that . . . conditions change radically with time. A "fifty-fifty" agreement with a foreign cor-

[14] Peter Gabriel, "Investment in the LDC," *Columbia Journal of World Business,* Summer, 1966, pp. 112–113. Quoted by permission.

poration that is seen as highly advantageous today, in comparison with previous arrangements in the same country or concurrent deals in other countries, will look intolerably onerous if other countries successfully bargain for 75% tomorrow. Moreover, both the need for and the uniqueness of the contribution made possible by a given foreign investment are bound to be vitiated by the very process of industrial development it was typically called in to assist.

It is not surprising, therefore, that host governments should continually be tempted to try to renegotiate or unilaterally alter existing contracts and long-term arrangements with foreign investors, or to revoke or "reinterpret" laws and regulations affecting them. Governments in the less-developed countries are subject to severe pressures to extract the best possible deal from the foreign businessman, even if it means taking liberties with specific contracts made or general promises given. It may be a matter of sheer economic necessity. In times of desperate foreign-exchange shortages, guarantees of free profit remission are more easily suspended than imports of essential goods. It may be a matter of political survival for incumbent governments, or of redeeming campaign pledges for newly elected governments. It is easier to marshal popular support by squeezing additional levies out of the foreigner on grounds of alleged "exploitation" than by acknowledging responsibility for domestic fiscal problems or failures. And there are the pressures from local business interests for protection from "unfair competition" unleashed by the allegedly more powerful foreign firm, or for license to participate in industries which the foreigner may have pioneered in the economy.[15]

The policy implications of these long- and short-term shifts in interests and power relations are clear, though by no means simple to achieve. A company must adopt a reasonably flexible attitude toward the terms of its relationships in a host country. This does not mean that legal contracts should be viewed as meaningless, for they are not. They are in themselves a part of the power structure, providing to the companies some degree of strength in any negotiation situation. The key point is that they are not to be regarded as absolutes which can be rigidly enforced even if the conditions under which they are negotiated change notably. This is an intellectually sound point and one which has now been proved realistic in sufficient cases to be validated. But for Western managements it has proved an extremely difficult point of view to accept because of the obsession of the Western mind with the letter

[15] *Ibid.*, pp. 114–115.

of the law, reinforced by nationalism and by real concern for the welfare of investments.[16] Thus the problem for management adds up to the need both to assess accurately the changes in circumstances and to achieve in its own thinking an effective degree of flexibility.

A BROADER PERSPECTIVE

The discussion in this chapter has concentrated on the manner in which nationalism, national interests, and the multinational firm interact in the types of situations normally encountered in international business. Viewing these on a current basis and with recognition of the effects of recent forms of change over time, we have evolved a conceptual framework which is meaningful in the environment which generally prevails in the free world today—a mixture of private- and public-enterprise economies functioning with a modicum of respect for property rights and continuity of responsible government. In this environment the resolution of conflicts by the process of negotiation based on power relationships along the lines presented here is, in fact, functioning and may, therefore, be regarded as viable.

A thoughtful student of history must, however, ask whether the environmental characteristics upon which the resolution process rests are assured. We must recognize that the compromises resulting from the present power balance are far from satisfactory to either side. Many multinational firms feel that their interests and those of their parent nations have suffered severely from the encroachments of foreign governments. But the dissatisfaction among the host nations is far greater, particularly in the tremendous body of accumulated resentment among the less developed countries against the industrial countries and their companies. They harbor a strong feeling that the industrialized countries have maltreated them in the past and are still trying to hold them back and milk their economies. For the most part, these feelings are

[16] A striking example of this attitude was provided by a review written by a businessman of Richard Robinson's book in which his advocacy of a flexible attitude toward contracts was sharply criticized. See John W. Scott, "A Critical Review of Intellectual Treason," *Business Abroad*, Aug. 10, 1964, pp. 30–31.

held in check by national political leaders who, recognizing their dependence on Western capital and skills, have been willing to work within the environmental constraints assumed in this chapter. But from time to time, the feelings break out in convulsions like those in Cuba and Indonesia, with foreign business swept under by a fundamental change in the environmental conditions.

In principle, this type of development is still consistent with the power-balance concept. The difference, as compared with the approach taken throughout the chapter, is that the great reserve powers of the host nations in their ultimate sovereignty have been brought to play. Such eventualities suggest the possibility of even more radical changes in the environmental constraints. What, for example, would be the effect if all of the less developed countries agreed among themselves to demand that the industrial countries supply them with capital and skills on modest economic terms and with no control (i.e., no further establishment of subsidiaries in their countries) and that they would enforce this with the same type of collective political power (with military force in reserve) which countries like Cuba and Indonesia have exercised internally? We have already in the United Nations Conference on Trade and Development (UNCTAD) the beginnings of such collective action by the less developed countries. So far, their demands and approach to pressing them have been modest and quite within the environmental constraints assumed in this chapter. But it is not impossible that, if conditions in their economies do not improve rapidly enough and political pressures grow, a more radical approach might appear.

These notes are necessarily hazy and their message may in fact prove in time to have been irrelevant. But in a century which has seen such massive areas as Russia and China pass through radical changes in political-economic environment, one must recognize the possibility that other large areas may experience equally extreme changes.

The implications of all this for corporate strategy are equally uncertain. The firm as a small social entity must, by and large, relate its strategy to the environment in being at any one time with modest efforts to adjust its decisions to reasonably expectable changes in the environmental constraints. If the environmental constraints are in themselves inconsistent with overall social needs, it can do little to change them. That sort of adjustment is essentially the job of major social institutions like national governments and the United Nations. It may well participate as a *citizen* in the efforts of the governing bodies, but its individual influence is small. On an overall basis, therefore, the question which must remain unanswered is whether the processes of accommodating conflicts of interests among nations at the governmental level can evolve satisfactorily within the present general pattern. If not, then the ground rules upon which the conceptual framework for corporate strategy have been evolved here may be radically altered.

SUMMARY

A mutuality of interests between the multinational firm and host nations in processes of the transmission of resources and innovation in host societies is the *sine qua non* for international business. But some degree of conflict is inevitable in these processes. This chapter has added to the conceptual framework an approach to understanding and dealing with the conflict component of the processes. The conflicts have been considered as composed of two parts. First, an area of valid conflict in which soundly based positions on each side are mutually exclusive. Second, an extension of the area of conflict because of misconceptions as to what is the true interest of each arising from ignorance, prejudice, and other causes. Prominent among these causes are the nationalistic attitudes of the participants. There is an inherent conflict in the xenophobic reaction of the members of the national we-group toward the multinational firm which, by definition, attempts at least to some degree to penetrate their society with objectives of profit and control. These reactions add a component of illogical emotion to discussions of conflicts of interests which might otherwise be dealt with in a relatively objective manner.

The resolution, or at least minimization, of these problems in international business has been found to lie along two main lines. First, there is the effort to achieve maximum accommodation among the interests of the parties. This involves efforts to reduce the extent of the misconceptions of interest on the part of the management of the multinational firm, parent-country government officials, and host-country nationals. An important component of this process is the effort to minimize nationalistic emotional reactions in the interests of greater rational discussion of issues by measures ranging from avoidance of heated public debate to broadening and effectively utilizing the third-culture groups which are most capable of objective action. Second, the resolution of the hard core of valid conflict must inevitably come through negotiation based on relative economic and political power relationships. The power available to the multinational firms and to host countries varies greatly from situation to situation and over the course of time. Thus a flexible approach to corporate policies affected by national interests and nationalism is required.

Chapter Five
The Global Business Strategy

Up to this point we have been considering the problems of a multi-national firm on a bicountry (host country–parent country) basis. But this basis is clearly too limited for a conceptual framework for the strategy of the multinational firm which characteristically is involved in many countries. We must, therefore, broaden the scope of analysis to consider the opportunities and problems of multi-country operation.

UNIFICATION VERSUS FRAGMENTATION

Just as the effect of an intervening border between two nations provided the central focus for the conceptual framework in the bicountry analysis, so here the intervention of many national borders is the logical point of departure. What fundamental effects do their existence have on the strategy of the multinational firm? Although many effects can be itemized, one central theme recurs, that is, their tendency to push the firm toward adaptation to the diversity of local environments which leads toward fragmentation of operations. But there is a natural tendency in a single firm toward integration and uniformity which is basically at odds with fragmentation. Thus the central issue which emerges from examination of an assortment of specific aspects of multination strategy is the conflict between unification and fragmentation [1]—a close-knit opera-

[1] The term *unification* is not perfect for the purposes intended in this chapter, but it seems to be the most appropriate word available in the English language. *Integration* would fit some aspects of the subject, but it does not go far enough to encompass the standardization and uniformity which are intended by the unification idea. That is, one can have substantial integra-

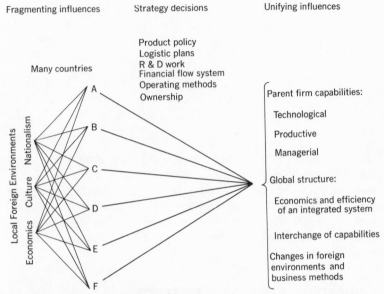

Figure 5.1 Fragmentation versus unification.

tional strategy with similar foreign units versus a loosely related, highly variegated family of activities. This issue, as summarized in Figure 5.1, will be examined first as it appears in the major aspects of multicountry activities, shown in the center of the figure, and then in broader terms bearing on the role of the multinational corporation in world society.

It should be emphasized that the discussion in this chapter con-

tion in the structuring of activities, even though they may be quite diverse in character. *Centralization* is also pertinent in some sections, but in common parlance it pertains only to certain types of structural features such as decision making and production sources and not to others like the flow of product know-how from one subsidiary to another, so it is not adequate. Similar alternatives to *fragmentation* have been considered. On balance, it appears that unification and fragmentation provide the best available means of expressing the basic idea of this chapter. The reader is cautioned, however, to use them here according to the meaning which emerges from the discussion in the chapter rather than being limited by an initial dictionary definition.

cerns the operational processes in the firm, not its organizational processes. The unification-fragmentation issue is also pertinent to the latter and will be considered accordingly in Chapter 6. However, the strategy employed in the operational processes is not necessarily the same as that of the organizational processes. That is, it is quite possible for a firm with a high degree of unification of decision making in headquarters to deliberately choose various operational patterns of a fragmented nature which appear to be more effective than unified approaches. Likewise, a company in which decision making is very fragmented, with much authority delegated to field units, might have a unified approach on some aspects of operations because the field managers found such an approach beneficial. As a practical matter, one does observe that in many companies the pattern in both respects is similar; and this is natural, for the organizational pattern reinforces the operational and vice versa. Indeed, from time to time in this chapter, elements of fragmentation in organizations will be noted as variables favoring fragmentation of operations. But in an objective analysis such as we are pursuing here, the two must be recognized as separate characteristics.

To lay a preliminary foundation for this discussion, we will review the main influences for fragmentation and unification shown in Figure 5.1. The fragmenting influences indicated on the left encourage managements to tailor operations in each country (A, B, C, etc.) to its unique combination of economic, cultural, nationalistic, and other characteristics. Effective relations with the host society, as discussed in Chapter 3, frequently argue for policies and practices which conform to the particular system of economic and interpersonal relations of the local environment. The satisfaction of national interests and minimization of the emotional resistances of nationalism, considered in Chapter 4, favor approaches which are oriented toward localism rather than global unity. If these influences were given full play, the ultimate result would be a family of foreign units, each showing a relation to the others but with substantial diversity among them in a number of phases of operations. As the discussion so far in this book has indicated, there is much to be said for significant adaptation to the conditions in each country so that the fragmentation strategy has its merits.

The unifying influences shown on the right, however, are a

strong counterforce composing in sum a substantial portion of the basic rationale for the existence of the multinational firm and the source of a considerable part of its competitive advantage. There is, in the first instance, the strength embodied in the various capabilities available within the parent company, notably its technological competence, its managerial know-how, and its productive facilities. As we saw in Chapter 2, comparative advantages in the skills and capital resources these represent are typically the main economic bases from which the activities of the multinational firm arise. In general, these capabilities are at their peak effectiveness when applied to the company's established pattern of activities. They can, therefore, be most effectively drawn upon to strengthen the operations of overseas units when the activities of the units fall in the same pattern.

Second, like any large enterprise, the multinational firm must capitalize as fully as possible on the potential advantages of size in its global span as compared to strictly local, smaller firms. The possibilities for economies and greater efficiency available to it lie largely in capabilities for specialization of activities in individual units with substantial interchange among them and are therefore dependent upon a high degree of uniformity in the activities of the units composing the structure. Likewise, the potential benefits from the large financial capabilities of a global organization are generally realized most effectively in a system with a high degree of unification of planning and operations.

Third, there is the apparently reasonable assumption indicated in Chapter 3 that all nations as they arrive at advanced stages of industrial development will have substantially similar characteristics. This assumption provides management with a sound conceptual basis for working toward greater uniformity of activities in many countries around the world as opposed to the assumption that existing diversities among nations have an expectation of permanence. Unlike the first two points, this one is not in itself an argument for unification. That is, it does not in its own logic provide any direct gain in effectiveness for a particular policy or action. Rather it is a counterargument to some of the fragmenting influences shown on the left of Figure 5.1. Thus in any given situation where there is a rough balance between the local environmental factors favoring a fragmentation approach and elements in the multinational corporation structure favoring unification, the assumption of change in foreign business systems weakens the force of the former to the benefit of the latter. So, even though it is not a positive force in itself, the general process of evolution of reasonably similar modern industrial societies reinforces unification in the strategies of multinational firms.

There can obviously be no clear-cut choice between the unification and fragmentation approaches to strategy. The problem is essentially one of balance as these considerations apply in a number of individual decisions. We will consider their implications here with respect to six major areas of strategy: product policy, logistic plans, distribution of R & D work, financial flow systems, operating methods, and ownership.

PRODUCT POLICY

Fragmentation-unification considerations play a vital part in determining product policy for international business. Differences in income levels, cultural characteristics of consumers, climate, and other market factors constantly pull in the direction of products specialized according to individual countries. The unification factors, however, are persuasive arguments for holding to worldwide standardization of product lines.

The fragmentation influences have varying degrees of force, depending upon their nature and the types of products involved. Most compelling are environmental conditions which critically affect the functional utility of products, with cultural and other aspects having lesser but still significant influence. For example, where 220-volt power systems are employed, electrical appliances must be adapted to them, and the steering wheels of automobiles must be placed on the right or left side according to the traffic laws of each country if a company wishes to achieve good market acceptance. From these obvious cases we move off into a spectrum of situations in which the degree of compulsion for local adaptation from environmental features varies with the element of change in foreign societies often a prominent factor.

Refrigerators provide an interesting example. The 15-cubic-foot refrigerator is standard in the United States where housewives use it for storage of a large variety and amount of food and where families are affluent enough to be able to afford its luxury. In Europe, kitchens are smaller, housewives shop more frequently, and the cost of a refrigerator is a greater burden because incomes are lower. These factors have combined to establish a 6-cubic-foot refrigerator as standard. In Latin America, although the same factors prevailing in Europe apparently argue for small refrigerators, companies found until a few years ago that the main demand was for larger, U.S.-style units. This preference might be accounted for by the higher temperatures, but in the main it seems to have arisen from attitudinal causes. At the outset only the well-heeled upper classes could afford refrigerators, and they bought the U.S. models not only because they were the ones the U.S. companies could most readily supply to them, but also because among many Latin Americans imitation of U.S. standards of material life style is viewed with favor. Subsequently, capacity to buy refrigerators appeared among the middle classes. From a practical viewpoint, they might have been better off buying smaller units. But, in fact, refrigerators became a status symbol, and many middle-class families felt impelled to buy the bigger units. More recently, the smaller models have gained a larger market share, perhaps because in the lower economic levels the utilitarian-economic factors are more compelling and perhaps because cars and television sets have superseded the refrigerator as prime status symbols.

For each product the nature of the fragmentation influences will differ. One can identify certain patterns in the ways in which they affect products—for example, according to their convenience and labor utilization features or their requirements for service.[2] But extended analysis along these lines is not essential for our present purposes. It is sufficient to observe that a company seeking maximum market penetration in each country will attempt to adjust to assorted local environmental conditions. Some of the conditions are so compelling that they must be accepted. Most, however, are to varying degrees less compelling so that the company has a practical choice between adapting to them with a fragmented product policy or seeking a more unified policy by counteracting

[2] For a further discussion of this subject, see the chapter "Product Policy" in Fayerweather, *International Marketing*, Prentice-Hall, Inc., Englewood Cliffs, N.J., 1965, pp. 49–61.

the fragmenting influences with offsetting approaches like persuasion through advertising or use of its economic advantages.

The persuasion approach often finds support in the tendency of foreign countries to move toward some approximation of a uniform model of an advanced industrial society. In the refrigerator case, for example, it would appear that aside from some climatic differences, the basic utilitarian features of the device have a certain recurring relationship to the economics of human life which would support uniformity of product patterns among peoples at similar levels of economic development. If such tendencies are valid, then efforts to persuade peoples to move away from their present localized preferences have an underlying support.

The economic advantages all relate to the unifying influences shown on the right in Figure 5.1. They are the means through which a multinational firm with reasonable standardization in its worldwide product line can either produce products at lower costs or generate a stronger selling program than a company following a fragmented policy.

First, there are the advantages to the foreign units of being able to draw on the technological capabilities of the parent company. If the units wander off into product areas in which they have no technical support beyond their own limited resources, they are relatively weaker in a competitive world. Richard Robinson describes a somewhat extreme but certainly illustrative case in the experience of Minneapolis-Moline, which got into the manufacture of septic tanks in Argentina and textile machinery parts in Turkey because import restrictions cut off imports of components for manufacture of tractors.[3] The foreign units could not benefit from technological support from the parent in such product lines, so they were in effect on the same competitive level in this regard as local national firms.

Second, for all but the simplest types of products, some drawing upon the productive capacities of the parent concern or of other foreign units as part of an integrated world production system is beneficial to individual foreign units. In the typical case a foreign subsidiary will turn out a number of end products, but many of

[3] Richard D. Robinson, *Cases in International Business,* Holt, Rinehart and Winston, Inc., New York, 1962, pp. 79, 91.

these will contain components imported from other company factories, usually from the United States. This sort of structure has underlying logics which were discussed in the analysis of methods of transmitting resources in Chapter 2, so ability to integrate component and end-product production in various countries is important to the basic economic strength of many firms. If such a system is to operate most efficiently, the product lines must be essentially the same. Likewise, if the opportunities to benefit by specializing production in different countries in an integrated logistic plan are to be realized along the lines to be discussed in the next section, there must again be a uniformity of product lines.

Finally, the opportunities for benefiting by the interchange of knowledge among various units around the world are dependent upon the units engaging in essentially the same type of business. For example, if company X introduces a particular new food product in Mexico and learns how to promote it effectively, the company can then apply this same know-how in introducing the identical product in other Latin American countries. The approach in each country will, of course, have to be different to some degree, but the company will have a substantial initial advantage over the position it would be in if it started off with quite different products in each country each time. One manufacturer of home appliances had such an experience in Brazil a few years ago. Hampered by import restrictions, the company took on several locally made products, including baby carriages, and even started selling life insurance policies to hold its sales organization together. On a short-term basis these expedients had a certain operational logic, but the potentials for the transfer of know-how from other parts of its international organization to help the Brazilian unit were much lower in these product lines than in the normal company fields. The marketing experts in the home office would have been hard put to advise the Brazilians on how to increase sales of insurance policies.

These arguments are generally so persuasive that most companies do have essentially the same product lines throughout the world. They are considerably less convincing, however, when applied to minor product variations to fit needs of individual markets —for example, modest changes in styling or of size of units or perhaps even of quality standards. Within limits, there is no significant loss of the gains from parent technological assistance or the exchange of knowledge among units with this type of product variation. It does, however, limit the amount of component and product exchange that is possible within the international structure. The significance of this will obviously depend upon the nature of the product line. In office machinery, for example, it is a real disadvantage; whereas for cosmetics or other simple consumer products, it probably has little relevance.

LOGISTIC PLANS

As the foregoing suggests, the logistic plan of the international business is a key phase of the unification-fragmentation strategy. The logistic plan of a company is the system of production units and flows of products by which it supplies its markets. The discussion of resource differentials and flows in Chapter 2 dealt in effect with logistic plans for companies operating in two countries. The same ingredients provide the underlying bases for the development of a multination logistic plan.

The ideal in such a plan is to achieve the most profitable combination of flows among countries. Since there are within the six major categories of resources (natural resources, labor, capital and technological, managerial, and entrepreneurial skills) a multitude of subcategories, each with its own pattern of international differentials, a planner equipped with a computer could work out a very complex logistic scheme to achieve optimum economic results of unification.[4] Figure 5.2 indicates in simplified form the type of scheme which might be forthcoming from this type of anal-

[4] Despite the apparent suitability of this area for operations research methodology, little effort has actually been made by scholars. No significant published work on the subject has appeared. The only strong effort known to the author is an unpublished doctoral dissertation: David P. Rutenberg, "Stochastic Programming with Recourse for Planning Optimal Flexibility in Multinational Corporations," University of California, Berkeley, Calif., 1967. Dr. Rutenberg presents an operations research approach to product design and production planning as a combined problem (and similar schemes for ownership patterns and for pricing and advertising). Although his mathematical model does not contain all the variables affecting decisions, it incorporates enough to demonstrate the dimensions of the analysis which would be required if the approach were put into application.

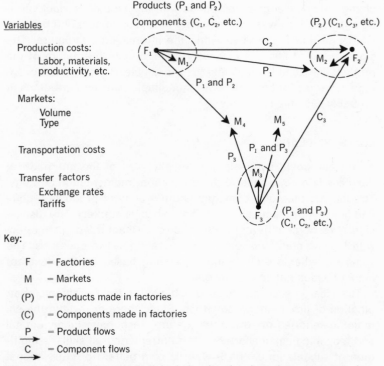

Figure 5.2 Sample model of logistic planning based on economic factors.

ysis. The company in this case is assumed to be operating in five countries. A comparison of wages, productivity, and other production cost factors matched against the volume of demand for different types of products in individual markets and consideration of transportation costs and transfer factors (tariffs and exchange rates) leads to locating factories in three countries: F_1, F_2, and F_3. Two of these are self-contained plants and the third, F_2, is partially an assembly operation dependent upon F_1 and F_3 for some components. The "sourcing" of the components is dependent upon costs, C_2 being available at lowest cost from F_1 and C_3 from F_3. The sourcing of end products is dependent upon costs and the demand in each market. F_1, for example, appears to be generally the lowest cost supply point, so M_4 obtains P_1 from there rather than F_3. On the other hand, it does buy P_3 from F_3 because F_1 does not make it.

The potentials of the pure economic model are substantially limited by the distortions introduced by government actions which have very commonly been directed toward national self-sufficiency rather than maximizing international trade flows. There have been sufficient obstacles and uncertainties so that multinational companies have often followed a fragmented approach, thinking of each overseas plant as a supply point for only the market in its own country, the major exceptions being plants in England or Canada which served other countries in the British Commonwealth.

Environmental factors are now more favorable to intercountry flows. We have the evolution of a number of regional groupings in which barriers between countries are being lowered, notably the European Common Market and the European Free Trade Area, but also including promising areas in Central America and Latin America. And with the pressing need to earn foreign exchange in many countries, U.S. subsidiaries are being encouraged to undertake export operations. There is a growing feeling among those concerned with economic growth of the less developed countries that the expansion of exports of labor-intensive manufactured goods can be a major factor in further progress. As suggested in Chapter 2, the increasing participation of multinational firms in the reverse flow of resources from these countries is a quite likely development for the future.

Thus international firms find it sound strategy to move toward somewhat more complex logistic plans. They are still conservative in their approach, recognizing that the risks of extensive dependence on intercountry flows remain significant and perhaps not worth the fairly modest economic gains available, particularly where they require substantial capital commitments in production facilities. The possibilities of imposition of barriers to trade will be ever present so long as we have independent nation-states. Sometimes actions will be forced because of the existing poorly developed methods of achieving international economic adjustments among nations, even though they are committed to reducing trade barriers. For example, in 1963 Italy imposed restrictions against imports including those from other EEC countries, in

1964 Britain placed a surtax of 15 percent on manufactured imports including those from her EFTA partners, and in 1968 France took special measures restricting trade because of the crisis created by a national strike. In each case, severe balance-of-payment problems forced the hand of governments whose basic policies were to favor freer trade. In other cases, we may anticipate restrictions arising from essentially protectionist sentiment not only among the newly industrializing nations but even among advanced countries—the threat of assorted import quotas in the 1967 U.S. Congress being a prime example. The managements of multinational firms have therefore a legitimate cause for concern, and it may be sound practice to have plants in a somewhat greater number of countries than would be justified to achieve the optimum benefits of rationalization at a given moment.

To these general limitations must be added other factors including product characteristics and ownership factors in specific cases which work toward a further fragmentation of the logistic plan. If, as noted above, products must be varied substantially among countries for cultural or other reasons, the feasibility of intercountry flows is naturally reduced. There is a wide range of products, including staples like gasoline and machinery products like trucks, for which this factor should not be of great importance so long as a company sticks to the same product line in each country. Its chief influence is on more variable consumer lines like foods and on companies whose foreign units have been allowed to move into diverse product fields.

The ownership question is relevant because it limits the flexibility of management in making advantageous shifts in logistic plans and also because of antitrust considerations. If a company owns fully all of its foreign units, it can shift production of particular components or end products from one to another largely on the basis of overall corporate objectives. But if there are local investors as partners in one or more of the units, then their interests have to be considered. Presumably, a partner in a joint venture would not be pleased if the company proposed that the production in his country be cut back and output shifted to another country. The antitrust problem stems from the prevailing view that under U.S. law joint ventures should be treated as independent companies, whereas wholly owned subsidiaries are an integrated part of a company. Thus there is no legal deterrent to logistic plans for an integrated company under which the pattern of supply for the world is carefully laid out and controlled by the parent organization. But such a scheme worked out by a U.S. company with a group of foreign firms in which it has a partial interest may be subject to legal action as a form of restraint of trade.

The opportunities and limitations in developing international logistic systems may be illustrated by two cases.

First, Robert Valtz has described the problems of Universal Manufacturing and Control Co. (UMCC) in achieving some rationalization of its European operations.[5] The company made heavy machinery for manufacturing and construction and industrial process control equipment. Since World War II it had built plants in nine European countries. Cultural differences and other fragmentation influences provide little initial pressure in such a situation against centralized manufacture of individual products for several countries. Yet most UMCC products were made in three to six countries, and three products were made in all nine countries.

The main cause of this fragmentation was the level of tariffs which ran from 10 to 20 percent. Even though unit labor costs were only 40 percent of those in the United States, manufacturing costs were 105 to 115 percent of U.S. levels. According to one estimate, the latter would be cut to 75 percent or 85 percent if production of each item were centralized. These figures suggest the company was already tolerating somewhat greater cost disadvantages from fragmentation than the tariff levels would justify and with the rapid reduction in tariffs within EEC and EFTA the economic considerations favored rationalization.

It appeared, however, that other factors were strong deterrents to action. Even though the products should have been uniform among countries, UMCC found that the management in each country had made small modifications to suit the desires of local customers. The company's public and government relations might suffer from breaking relations with various local suppliers or the loss of the "Made in——" sales image when products were imported rather than produced locally. Although no complications of shared

[5] Robert C. K. Valtz, "The Case of the Multiplant Manufacturer," *Harvard Business Review,* March–April, 1964, pp. 12–30. The name of the company is disguised.

local ownership were present, a somewhat related deterrent appeared in the vested interest of the managers in each country who resisted rationalization which would deprive them of much autonomy. And in the background of all this were the uncertainties of trade relations among the countries—the halting efforts at agreement between EEC and Britain and the other EFTA countries and the risk of obstacles such as the Italian and British cases cited above. Thus we can see that even in a product field and a geographic area where movement toward an economically rational logistic scheme is apparently most logical, the practicalities of achievement are restricted.

The second case is the Singer Company. In the establishment of foreign factories, Singer had through the early 1950s held fairly well to an economically rational logistic scheme. It was supplying most markets from a few large, efficient plants—one in Canada exporting to much of Latin America and another one in Scotland serving many European countries, Africa, and other areas.[6] Some fragmentation had evolved in Europe under the influence of tariffs with plants in France, Italy, and Germany, but each of these markets was large enough so that quite economic production was possible. Substantially less economic, however, was local production which was being forced on the company by governments of developing nations including Mexico, Brazil, and Turkey. There was every indication that these pressures would continue. In fact the company had already lost the large Indian market because it had failed to set up a plant, and a local firm had taken the market over behind a protective wall of import restrictions. Thus a steady shift toward greater fragmentation of the logistic plan among the less developed countries seemed inevitable. In Europe, the advent of the Common Market resulted in some shift in the other direction with specialization of production of individual products among the factories in the EEC countries.

A major factor in this story is the role of the Japanese sewing machine industry from which Singer had been excluded after World War II by government restrictions. During the 1950s Japanese manufacturers, working with extremely low labor costs,

---

[6] For further description, see the Singer Manufacturing Company cases in Fayerweather, *Management of International Operations,* McGraw-Hill Book Company, New York, 1960, pp. 541–547, 578–587.

made tremendous gains in world markets, providing Singer and European firms with very stiff competition, especially in lower-cost models. After losing a significant portion of its world market share, Singer, by rigorous efforts, was able to turn out machines in Europe at prices close to those of the Japanese. With its superior sales organization and reputation, it was more or less holding its own in the mid-fifties in those markets where it met the Japanese in open competition. Still the company was anxious to establish a production base in Japan. In 1953, Singer made an agreement with a Japanese producer, Pine Manufacturing Co., for a 50 percent interest with provision of further loan capital and technological assistance. The proposal blew up a storm of nationalistic resistance, fanned by the other Japanese manufacturers who feared Singer competition. So the government refused to approve the deal. Singer decided to go ahead anyway, but without government approval it could not repatriate earnings from Pine. Thus, although the Japanese factory potentially could serve as a valuable link in the logistic scheme as a source of low-cost products, the benefits to the company from using it were sharply limited. Not only did it have the problem of mixed ownership, but there was no telling when, if ever, it could receive in the parent firm such gains as might acrue from supplying markets from this source.

The effect of these problems is illustrated by the situation of a strikingly similar sewing machine company bearing the disguised name, International Manufacturing Company, described in another case.[7] In 1962 IMC was facing severe competition from the Japanese in Africa. It could obtain machines from company factories in Italy, Canada, and Brazil at relatively low prices, but its lowest quotation (about 30 percent below the others) was from a 50-percent-owned Japanese joint venture. Only the latter would be clearly competitive with the prices of IMC's Japanese competitors. Despite the apparently strong cost arguments favoring the Japanese source, IMC seemed very anxious to draw on the Italian plant instead. Although the case does not explicitly say so, analysis of its content strongly suggests that the problems of profit repatriation and management flexibility involved in procurement from the Japanese joint venture were the key deterrents.

[7] Edmund P. Learned et al., *Business Policy,* Richard D. Irwin, Inc., Homewood, Ill., 1965, pp. 1036–1041.

DISTRIBUTION OF R & D WORK

Strategy in the distribution of research and development work within a multinational organization is properly part of the subject matter of this chapter, although the fragmentation-unification issue is not so closely balanced with it as with other aspects of strategy. It must be emphasized at the outset that unification here does not necessarily mean centralization in one country. In fact, the more sophisticated companies are tending to develop R & D programs in which work is allocated to different countries according to the availability of scientific competence, salary levels, and other factors. The broad survey of R & D work in multinational firms conducted by David Hertz brings out substantial complications in coordinating an integrated but geographically decentralized program of this nature, especially in achieving communications across distance and culture gaps.[8] But this approach is well developed in some companies like International Telephone and Telegraph, which has a highly sophisticated European research organization [9] and General Motors whose small-car development has centered in Europe. Thus, in speaking of unification, we mean an R & D program in which projects are either centralized or allocated among countries and coordinated to compose an integrated scheme.

The arguments for a primary emphasis on unification of the R & D system are overwhelming. It is inconceivable that a company should duplicate its basic research and product-development activities in all or even several foreign countries. The economies of concentrating research in limited locations where facilities are well developed are fundamental to the competitive advantage of the multinational firm. The fragmentation-unification issue therefore appears in weighing the merits of relatively modest degrees of fragmentation.

Three pulls in the direction of fragmented R & D activities are

[8] David B. Hertz, "R. and D. as a Partner in World Enterprise," *European Business,* October, 1967, pp. 24–28.

[9] John B. Bennett, an ITT executive, describes his company's approach in "Sizing Up the Cost of Research and Engineering Abroad," *Management Review,* June, 1961, pp. 49–55.

apparent. First, there are local market conditions which argue for on-the-spot study to develop products for maximum local acceptance. To the extent that fragmentation of products has been justified on its own merits, there is a sound argument for developing these product variations locally as part of a unified R & D plan. The debatable area therefore lies in the extent to which local efforts go beyond such specific allocation of effort to study product innovations which are already the subject of study in other company units.

Second, the presence in many countries of individuals capable of R & D contributions offers an opportunity which a multinational firm will often be wise to grasp. For example, able research chemists are scattered throughout the world. A chemical firm seeking to build a strong R & D organization might be inclined to hire and utilize these people wherever it could find them. At a minimum, such a policy may be supported as a defensive counter to the prospect that the same people will appear in the laboratories of competitors who have adopted a fragmentation strategy.

This sort of local employment of scientists in several countries might be made an effective part of a unified scheme by allocating different areas of investigation to each country. But this is often not the most efficient way to incorporate them into a unified system because of the communications difficulties and other shortcomings of a decentralized program. The shortcomings are especially significant when only one or two scientists in a relatively undeveloped country are involved. Such people are likely to be far less productive working in a local subsidiary than in a centralized research group with superior equipment and ready access to an advanced scientific community in one of the highly industrialized countries.

This leads us into the sensitive subject of the "brain drain," the flow of professional people from the less developed to the advanced countries and from Europe to the United States. Better salaries are a factor in this process, but studies have shown that the higher level of scientific work in the advanced countries coupled with superior research facilities offering greater professional opportunities are powerful attractions.[10] The loss of intellectural re-

[10] Thomas J. Mills, "Scientific Personnel and the Professions," *The Annals,* September, 1966, pp. 34–35.

sources of many countries is generally deplored, but the net effect of the process is subject to debate. There are those who believe that the scientist will be more productive in the advanced country, and all countries will benefit from the dissemination of this greater productivity. Applied to the R & D program of the multinational firm, all of this argues from recruiting scientists wherever they may be found and bringing them together in laboratories in the more advanced countries rather than following a fragmentation strategy simply because of the initial dispersed locations of the scientists.

Third, the influence of national interests and nationalism is a considerable factor in this area. Many countries are extremely sensitive about their technological dependence upon the most advanced industrial nations. As we have seen in Chapter 2, the transmission of superior skills is the main contribution of international firms. Given the overwhelming scientific lead of a few countries, the flow of skills and resultant dependency seems inevitable for the foreseeable future. But no matter how useful the relationship may be, it still is a cause of practical concern and emotional resentment in the skill-importing countries; so they express a strong desire to have multinational firms do more research in their countries. For example, in a study conducted by the National Planning Association, the magnitude of local research ranked as one of six major causes of resentment toward U.S. firms in Canada on a par with such other sore issues as ownership and use of local management personnel.[11]

The extent to which the greater efficiency and effectiveness of a unified scheme may weigh against national interest and nationalism influences depends very much on the types of analysis pursued in Chapter 4. Conceptually it would appear that the greatest power of most multinational firms resides in its R & D program, so it could not readily be forced to accede to local pressures on this count. On the other hand, the sensitivity of this subject is so great that good relations with national groups may be substantially advanced by modest concessions in an otherwise unsound shift toward fragmentation. Or to be quite specific, opening a small research laboratory may generate enough beneficial goodwill among

[11] John Lindeman and Donald Armstrong, *Policies and Practices of United States Subsidiaries in Canada*, National Planning Association, Washington, D.C., 1960, pp. 57–64.

local scientists, the government, and the public as a whole to compensate for some loss in direct research productivity as compared with an equal outlay in some other country as part of a unified R & D scheme.

The net effect of these various factors in company practice is indicated in the intensive study of foreign subsidiaries in Canada undertaken by A. E. Safarian. Roughly half of the subsidiaries from whom information on R & D effort was obtained reported no such expenditures.[12] About 80 percent of the balance reported that their R & D programs were largely coordinated with the parent-company work.[13] Thus only about 10 percent of the companies in this group would appear to be following a basically fragmented strategy. Safarian's data do not permit us to determine fine variations in the nature of the strategies. However, the impression one gains from his discussion is that in most cases the subsidiaries had been given significant opportunity to study both improvement of present products and development of new ones. In light of the relative similarity of the U.S. and Canadian markets, this would appear to be a tendency toward fragmentation, justified more by a desire to satisfy Canadian attitudes than by economic logics. That is, it would appear quite practical and probably more efficient to do all R & D work appropriate for Canada in U.S. facilities, as half the firms did. This can only be a tentative conclusion, however, subject to revision when further research is done. We would have to know, for example, whether the salary scales of the Canadian scientists were lower or whether in certain fields the scientific resources in Canada, both within the company and in the surrounding scientific community, were superior. If these elements were favorable, the concentration of work on specific projects in Canada might be sound as part of a unified scheme.

FINANCIAL FLOW SYSTEMS

The financial flow system encompasses all transfers of money within the multinational corporation, including transmission of

---

[12] A. E. Safarian, *Foreign Ownership of Canadian Industry,* McGraw-Hill Book Company, New York, 1966, p. 176.

[13] *Ibid.,* p. 187.

capital and various forms of income (sales income, licensing, royalties, management fees, interest, dividends, etc.). There are many specific financial decisions involved in the system, each based upon a variety of factors. For example, a choice between obtaining local capital by a stock issue or borrowing depends upon such considerations as the adequacy of the local capital market, the willingness of the host country to let the foreign firm use the local capital market, the financial strength of the subsidiary, and the relative costs of obtaining the capital. But the issue of fragmentation versus unification is ever present. The fragmentation approach argues for decisions which treat the foreign units largely as self-contained enterprises dealing with the parent company essentially as independent companies. The unification approach treats them in much the same manner as integrated segments of a domestic company with the financial decisions dominated by overall corporate considerations.

The local environmental influences favoring the fragmentation approach are strong enough so that most companies find it desirable to work through national corporate entities with discrete financial structures ranging from fully owned subsidiaries to independent licensees. Tax and other legal considerations within host nations generally favor segregation of each foreign unit, assuring that the rest of the multinational corporation is not entangled intimately with each unit's financial affairs. The one major exception to this generalization is the structure commonly found among U.S. extractive companies which integrate their foreign and domestic operations to benefit from depletion provisions of U.S. tax laws. But among other types of firms the common foundation for the financial flow system is a group of local national corporate entities.

The fragmenting influences work toward financial decisions directed toward the local interests of each of these units. Host governments, for example, favor the retention of earnings for further local development. They expect local units to "bargain" for the benefit of the host country against the parent in price, royalty, and other transactions. Competitors resent the access of multinational subsidiaries to world credit facilities and parent-company guarantees on local borrowing and press their governments to protect them by restrictions on the subsidiaries. Even the local management personnel are a fragmenting influence because they generally want to stand on their own feet, neither being overly dependent on the parent for help nor wishing to have their profits drained away for use elsewhere in the world. Indicative of their attitudes was the resentment generated in the British subsidiary of one company when that unit was required to borrow $16 million from local banks for construction while in the same year it had to remit $2.7 million, a large portion of its earnings, to the parent. The benefits to the corporation of its policy of maximizing the use of local debt capital were admitted by the subsidiary management. But they still would have preferred to be allowed to reinvest the local earnings rather than be saddled with a heavy debt load. Local participation in ownership of foreign units is a further fragmenting influence. Though the multinational firm may at times seek some overall corporate benefit at the expense of a joint-venture unit, on the whole the legal and moral obligations of such a partnership require that it be treated as a separate entity. Thus transfer pricing, management fees, and other financial arrangements with it must on the whole be based on arm's-length negotiation.

But the unifying influences are also forceful. At the outset, of course, there is the basic cohesion provided by the parent as the central source of capital with attendant ownership rights. In the performance of its obligations to its stockholders, the multinational corporation must perforce exercise a degree of central financial control. This factor has been given added weight in recent years by the growing practice of consolidating the financial statements of overseas units with those of the parent corporation. So long as the reports of the foreign units are not consolidated and overseas results appear only as dividend receipts and aggregate estimates of net foreign assets, the fragmented treatment of their finances is encouraged. But if through consolidation the changes in each unit are brought continuously into the mainstream of corporate financial reviews, thinking of them as part of an integrated whole is fostered.

But beyond this there are strong influences for unification arising from the potential economies and efficiencies of an integrated financial system. The differences in capital markets, taxation systems, government regulations, and other financial conditions around the world create numerous opportunities for corporations which are able to plan on a global rather than a strictly national basis. We enter here into a subject which can readily occupy a full book. It will suffice for our purposes to mention two illustrations.

First, there is the general concept of allocating profits among countries to optimize overall corporate gain. The most common practice under this heading is that of maximizing profits in low-tax or economically secure countries and minimizing them in countries with high taxes, insecure economies, and severe foreign-exchange restrictions. A multinational company can, by a judicious combination of intracompany prices, licensing fees, and administrative charges, plan so that it realizes the greater portion of its profits in certain countries. Carried too far, such practices are of course illegal for tax purposes. The U.S. government, for example, has successfully challenged some firms which endeavored to maximize profit accumulation outside the United States by selling exports to subsidiaries at prices which seemed unduly low compared with prices charged to other customers.[14] But within the tolerance of legal and tax systems, companies may and do develop financial flow systems which minimize taxes and concentrate funds in the more secure countries.

James Shulman cites other reasons for deliberate profit allocation derived from his survey of intracorporate pricing practices.[15] In some instances, goods are shipped at unrealistically low prices from a well-established subsidiary to help a new subsidiary get started. Since in its initial years the latter would typically have losses, this practice may reduce taxes in the first country without a commensurate increase in the second. In addition, Shulman notes that by making a new operation appear more profitable, it is easier to persuade local lenders to supply capital for it.

Second, by utilizing the overall corporate financial strength, companies may advantageously adjust the portions of equity and debt in the financial structures of foreign units. Because of devaluation and other risks, companies generally prefer to maximize use of local debt capital abroad, especially in the weaker economies.

[14] Walter F. O'Connor, "Can Intercorporate Pricing Arrangements Avoid Being Upset by Section 482?" *The Journal of Taxation,* May, 1967, pp. 262–268.

[15] James Shulman, "When the Price Is Wrong—by Design," *Columbia Journal of World Business,* May–June, 1967, p. 72.

On its own, a foreign unit could only borrow, let us say, 60 percent of its capital requirements. But if the multinational corporation guarantees the credit of the foreign unit, then local lenders have far greater security, and it can borrow perhaps 80 percent of its needs. The financing of a $2.2 million expansion of the Australian subsidiary of one multinational firm is illustrative. The subsidiary borrowed $1.3 million from a local commercial bank, the parent guaranteeing the loan. The parent provided the balance of the $900,000 in equity. However, it obtained $670,000 of this by a loan from an Australian insurance company. In total, therefore, 90 percent of the capital was borrowed locally by virtue of unified planning and utilization of the total corporate financial power. This pattern of financing is subject to debate, as indicated in Chapter 2, but insofar as our present discussion is concerned it illustrates the potentials available in a unified financial system.

In contrast to the rather crude development of logistic planning, corporations have approached their international financial schemes with substantial effort toward refinement, seeking economic benefit with considerable sophistication. At first glance this might seem contrary to the observation made about the secondary interest in financial return indicated in Chapter 2. However, they are two rather different ideas. It is perfectly consistent for a company to minimize its financial commitment but to seek to maximize its return from what commitment it has made. This is essentially the policy stand which most companies have assumed. Because money as compared to plant and equipment is quite flexible and mobile, they have been willing to adopt whatever approaches seemed appropriate to maximize their return, investing substantially in the advice of financial consultants and tax lawyers and engaging in extensive controversies with tax authorities around the world in the process.

OPERATING METHODS

Operating methods encompass the wide range of practices and procedures by which a company accomplishes its business goals. The issue of unification versus fragmentation appears prominently in the worldwide pattern of operating methods because of the role of the multinational corporation in transmission of skills, considered in Chapter 2, and the societal forces discussed in Chapter 3.

Local national environments exert a strong pressure for fragmentation of operating methods. As the discussion in Chapter 3 indicated, there are substantial differences among countries in the way business is conducted, which are related to differences in economic, social, political, and cultural systems. Though it may often be desirable to attempt to introduce changes which depart from the prevailing business system, this system, supported by social sanctions, is a constant force favoring fragmentation.

In addition, internal pressure for fragmentation often comes from the attitudes of the management personnel of the foreign units supported by nationalism. If the local managers are competent and aggressive, they have a quite normal desire to exercise initiative by developing their own concept of suitable operating methods. In this they typically find moral support in local nationalism, even if they are nationals of the parent country.

Combining the influence of the local business system and the inclinations of the local management team, we have a natural centrifugal tendency which can readily lead to a highly fragmented pattern of operating methods. In some multinational organizations, one can see just such a pattern—a group of foreign units with some common characteristics but on the whole with great differences in marketing practices, personnel procedures, financial reports, and other operating methods.

This degree of fragmentation has its merits in fitting into foreign societies and satisfying local managers; however, there are significant arguments favoring unification of operating methods. Most prominent is the transmission of skills. As the discussion in Chapter 2 indicated, skills are generally the key components in the combination of resources which a multinational firm transmits abroad. Furthermore, it was apparent that many of these skills were intimately entwined with the ongoing processes of the business. Thus for the performance of one of its primary purposes the multinational firm benefits from a substantial degree of unification of operating methods. For example, let us consider the application of skill in new product management. A company might teach certain basic principles to foreign management teams and then guide them in applying the principles in assorted approaches developed according to the inclinations of the men on the spot. The parent-company managers would be more effective in facilitating the transmission of the skills, however, if they were applying directly the actual methods the company employs in the home country and variations on them learned in other countries. Some degree of adaptation to local conditions in each country will clearly be necessary, but the advantage to be gained by a unified structure of operating methods is clearly indicated.

Supporting and related to this basic objective of effective transmission of skills are considerations of interchange of personnel and organizational efficiency. In the next chapter these elements will be considered more fully. Suffice at this point to observe that much of the success of a multinational firm depends upon its worldwide management personnel. Their capabilities will be best utilized if they can be shifted from one foreign unit to another with a minimum of loss of time in adapting to new operating methods. Likewise the home office of the company can perform best if it has to cope with a minimum of variety in foreign units. The ideal situation would be a group of identical units so that personnel could move about with no lost effectiveness and the home-office competence was not dissipated by any effort to understand and deal with diversities. This ideal is obviously unattainable, but any feasible shift toward unification contributes in the desirable direction.

These arguments for unification are sufficiently persuasive so that most companies with controlled foreign units have substantially similar operating methods around the world, and there is a visible tendency toward more unification. In some companies with quite well-established systems, one finds the operating methods of foreign units prescribed in great detail. For example, a manufacturer of industrial equipment which has been operating successfully overseas for many years has spelled out a selling procedure which the foreign managements must follow. The local men still exercise some judgment in handling each customer, but the basic method of operation (embodying the company's refined marketing skill) is uniform around the world. In other companies, unification is not carried so far, but there appears to be a trend in that direction related to the toughening of international competitive conditions. A few years ago, it was possible in many countries for a multinational firm to prosper on the basis of some technological advantages and moderate effectiveness in applying other skills. As more companies have gone abroad and local industries have grown, however, competition has become more severe. Managements have found it essential, therefore, to apply their skills in operating methods as effectively as possible. This has led them to progressively greater integration and coordination of the skills of the parent organization and the foreign units, a process which in turn has moved toward a unification of methods. However, there is still of course substantial residual fragmentation to accommodate variations in local conditions.

The chief departures from this pattern are in those multinational organizations where the foreign units are not controlled by the parent firm. The pressures for fragmentation in the foreign units are obviously greater in these organizations, and the operating methods of licensees and joint ventures affiliated with multinational firms do typically vary considerably. Following the line of reasoning presented in Chapter 2, one must conclude that this is a significant weakness for such operations, assuming that the transmission of skills is the primary purpose of their affiliation with the multinational firm.

OWNERSHIP

The effect of policy on sharing ownership in foreign units with local partners has already been mentioned in phases of the unification-fragmentation issue discussed above. However, it is in itself a significant aspect of strategy deserving separate mention. The pressures of nationalism and local national interests pushing multinational corporations toward joint ventures were described in Chapter 4. Beyond these pressures the proponents of joint ventures argue their benefits as a means for bringing intimately into each foreign unit local nationals capable of understanding the environment of the host society and of directing the operations to fit its requirements. Thus the adoption of a policy of sharing ownership of the subsidiaries is inherently directed toward diversity in character of units. In this, it creates a vested interest which can be a block in attempts to achieve the benefits potentially available in a unified international structure. Specifically, as we have seen above, local ownership interests are a complicating factor in integrated logistic plans and financial flow systems, and they tend toward a fragmented pattern of operating methods which deters the transmission of skills.

These considerations are major factors in the general reluctance of multinational firms to enter into joint ventures. A recent study by the National Industrial Conference Board sums up the prevailing point of view.[16] Most business leaders accept the value of joint ventures as a means for minimizing the negative influence of nationalism, and many see positive advantages in bringing certain local resources into partnership in their enterprises. But they are also acutely conscious of the hazards of differences in management methods, divergent competitive objectives, and divided responsibility and authority. These problems may be minimized by careful selection of partners and advance policy and operational planning. But these measures are in themselves time-consuming, and there is usually some, and often considerable, residual loss of the potential benefits of unified management.

Although policies toward joint ventures vary greatly among companies, there are certain common patterns which stem largely from the emphasis placed on the factors we have discussed in different types of companies. The major automobile and petroleum companies have strongly resisted joint ventures because for them logistic flexibility is a prime consideration. For example, Ford invested heavily in the 1950s and 1960s to buy up minority shareholdings of local nationals in its Canadian, German, and English subsidiaries, including a $368 million purchase to achieve full control of the last in 1961.[17] Sales in the United States of cars made in the European subsidiaries from 1957 to 1967 are shown in the table on page 160.

Such sharp changes in logistic flows could be handled better in a system of fully owned units than in one with minority stockholders in each country, for whom major drops in export sales would be detrimental.

Among companies for whom international logistics are not so

[16] Karen Kraus Bivens and Enid Baird Lovell, *Joint Ventures with Foreign Partners,* National Industrial Conference Board, New York, 1965.

[17] Mira Wilkins and Frank Ernest Hill, *American Business Board: Ford on Six Continents,* Wayne State University Press, Detroit, Mich., 1964, p. 423.

	English	German
1957	17,062	29
1958	33,427	11,650
1959	42,413	6,570
1960	23,602	4,299
1961	8,660	667
1962	4,093	0
1963	3,702	0
1964	4,208	0
1965	4,887	0
1966	7,932	0
1967	15,992	0

sophisticated, there has been a greater receptivity to joint ventures, though the skill transmission and operating efficiency considerations still seem to weigh heavily against involvement with local partners. Westinghouse is an interesting case in point. Having worked for many years through licensees in which it had minority interests, Westinghouse launched a new program built on controlled subsidiaries in Europe in the 1960s.[18] The long history of difficulties in some of its earlier ventures like Industria Electrica de Mexico suggests that the company felt it could function more effectively if it was not impeded by local partnerships. Although there are some companies in this category which deliberately seek joint ventures, the majority are inclined to do so only when required by government regulations or where nationalistic pressures are so strong that it seems judicious to have a local ally.

Much greater receptivity to shared ownership is found among smaller firms which stand to gain more from the contributions of local partners and among firms where the disadvantages of joint ventures are not so significant. An excellent example of the latter type is Armco Steel Company, which has worked very successfully through minority participation in several foreign steel companies. There is little question of international logistic complications or competitive conflicts of interest in their operations which are largely confined to individual countries. The skills Armco provides

[18] "Westinghouse Now Goes All the Way," *Business Week*, June 29, 1963, pp. 49–52.

are essentially technological and thus easier to transmit than managerial and entrepreneurial skills, and they are dealing with large foreign firms which typically are well established and quite competent to absorb the skills.

THE STRUCTURE OF THE MULTINATIONAL CORPORATION

Product policy, logistic plans, distribution of R & D work, financial flow systems, operating methods, and ownership policy are all important aspects of the unification-fragmentation issue by themselves. But in sum they lead us to the broader question of the basic structure of the multinational corporation. Two extremes were indicated at the start of this chapter: first, a close-knit, well-integrated structure in which all the basic decisions we have been reviewing are made in the unification direction and, second, a loosely related, highly variegated family of enterprises in which the decisions are made in the direction of fragmentation. The former is essentially an extension on an international scale of the typical domestic industrial concern. The latter would appear as a group of independent national firms with quite diverse activities, tied together by licensing and similar arm's-length agreements and possibly by some exchange of capital, though with little ownership control exercised by one unit over another.

Looking at the nature of international enterprises today, one can readily see that there is a real question as to what type of structure we are moving toward. Elements of both of these extremes are present. Because they are accustomed to it at home, most firms have a natural bias toward the unified structure. But there is no reason to assume that it is clearly the best for international business. And indeed there are strong forces pulling in the other direction. It is extremely difficult to predict the outcome of a process of industrial evolution like this, but a few reflections on the forces at work will at least put the matter in perspective.

The fragmented structure appears to be favored by considerations of immediate operational effectiveness and organizational pressures. It seems clear that adaptation to local environmental conditions and giving way to host-country nationalism and national interests will, on a short-term basis, maximize the acceptability of a firm abroad and lead generally to the fullest realization of immediate operational potentials. The organizational problems due to distance and cultural and nationality differences, to be discussed in the next chapter, are also minimized over the short term by structures which permit autonomy and diversity among the field units. In addition, there are definite long-term strengths in the basic concept of fragmentation to the extent that it results in solidly integrating each foreign unit with the host society, counteracting the inherent conflict between the multinational firm and nationalism.

The unified structure, on the other hand, seems most suitable for performance of the role of cross-cultural agent of change and for the transmission of resources. For the most part it appears that the drive, coordination, continuity, economies, and other factors which contribute to the achievement of these missions are most effectively attained within a unified corporate organization.

Both of these sets of advantages are significant, but there would seem to be a fundamental logic in favor of the second. The main thrust of the fragmentation arguments is toward making the multinational corporation fit most comfortably into the host nation. This in a sense is a desirable objective, but it is essentially defensive, not positive or constructive. If, on the other hand, the unified structure is most effective for the introduction of change and transmission of resources to the host nation, then it makes a greater contribution. It would appear, therefore, that this sort of structure is more consistent with the distinguishing functions and characteristics of the multinational firm.

But such a general conclusion should not be interpreted to mean that international business will ultimately be conducted by large-scale carbon copies of integrated domestic industrial firms. Rather it is more likely that a different pattern will emerge in which the corporate structures will vary according to the situation of each industry and company. We have within domestic industry substantial variations in degrees of unification—auto companies which sell through dealers and a sewing machine company which has its own retail stores, aircraft makers which buy from many subcontractors and petrochemical firms which are largely self-sufficient for raw-material needs, and so forth. It seems quite reasonable to

economic institution. It seems safe to conclude at this point that the global company is useful as a part of world evolution. However, the ways in which it will be useful over the years and the characteristics which will best facilitate the performance of its role are by no means clear as yet.

By comparison, we have over the past fifty to seventy-five years developed a fairly clear concept of the role and values of the large, publicly owned, private corporation within a reasonably integrated and homogeneous nation-state. This concept incorporates aspects of capital formation, distribution of the benefits of ownership and control among the public, relations to government and public objectives, accomplishment of innovation and economic growth, and provision of work opportunity and benefits from employment.

Though we may carry some of the thinking based upon these concepts into the international arena, the multinational corporation functions in quite a different manner, and it is likely that a somewhat different set of concepts must be evolved concerning its role and future course of evolution. The one sure characteristic of the firm is its unity as compared to the complete separation of fully independent national companies. Thus presumably its distinctive contributions as a socioeconomic institution should derive from the capabilities of unity. This is not, of course, the same as saying that a unification approach to all aspects of operations is beneficial, for throughout the fragmentation-unification discussion we have simply been considering the degree and form in which the inherent unity of the corporation will be applied.

Taking the broader social-value viewpoint permits us, however, to reexamine each of these issues to determine whether the multinational corporation in pursuit of its objectives evolves strategies which are beneficial to society as a whole. This analysis brings to light a notable deficiency in world society today—the lack of a medium to determine and foster world interests. In Chapter 4 we could effectively analyze the relations between the multinational corporation and the interests of the individual nation-state because the latter are fairly well defined and effectively organized. But turning to the multicountry analysis in this chapter, we have been limited to discussing the diversities among nations because there is no really effective concept of world interests. We have the beginnings of the process in the United Nations, the World Bank,

expect that the international scene will be just as varied. The variations in this instance will be heavily influenced by the types of factors we have been discussing. That is, for example, if transmission of a sophisticated combination of skills continues to be an essential element in the international computer enterprises, they will remain highly unified structures. On the other hand, if food tastes remain quite distinctive among countries and the skills of convenience food technology and marketing in which the United States has been dominant are mastered by many other countries, then a fragmented structure for food companies might be expected.

The form which fragmented structures may take is yet another question. Because of the rapid spread of joint ventures, many people currently expect them to be a major feature of international business in the future. There is reason to doubt this, however. The operational weaknesses of joint ventures are clear. In decision making and implementation they seem to have inherent shortcomings as compared to companies under unified control. Over the long term, therefore, it would seem more likely that where fragmentation is advantageous, it will be accomplished by the emergence of a new structure of independent firms dealing at arm's length with each other. Thus we might expect that licensing agreements and even management contract arrangements would be more enduring than joint ventures. Thus the latter may be a useful but largely transitory phase in the evolution of multinational business. In fact, one can see some signs of this type of evolution under way in the present scene. On the one hand, many firms have entered into joint ventures which seemed initially of mutual advantage but have subsequently bought out the controlling interest from their partners to achieve the advantages of unified structures. On the other hand, there are situations in which local interests, often supported by their governments, have taken over progressively greater control from multinational firms, and it appears likely that they have the competence and strength to take full control ultimately. They may do it by expropriation but more likely, if the power relationships justify the host national position, the multinational firms will withdraw on some mutually agreeable basis.

Finally, we may pitch this discussion at a yet higher level by pondering on the role of the multinational corporation as a socio-

the International Monetary Fund, and so forth, but just a bare beginning.

Thus discussion at this level is extremely vague, but it may nonetheless be useful for multinational corporate strategists because the long-term viability of their approaches presumably will depend upon it. Take, for example, the capital-formation question. A unified corporate strategy may at times call for movement of investment funds from one part of the world to another and at other times for maximum use of local capital drawn forth in part by guarantees offered by the strength of the parent firm. National interest is clearly an important factor bearing on each alternative, the former making outside capital available to the country, the latter fostering internal capital formation. But what is the world interest? Will the world as a whole benefit more from one of these functions than the other? Or more to the point, assuming both are needed, for which is the multinational firm best suited? At first glance we might say the former, but this is not necessarily so. Perhaps its unique role lies in its capacity for global transmission of skills which provide foci for local capital formation and that anything which facilitates maximum performance of this role is in the best world interest. But this is a very cursory observation, which may be most convincing only in demonstrating how inadequately our views on such matters are thought out. Thus in opening up this further approach to the fragmentation-unification question, we can do little more than to emphasize the fact that the multinational corporation is already a world institution and that a conscious effort to think in terms of world social benefits is a movement in the right direction. Presumably this approach will lead to stress on those strategies in which the gains from unity are optimized.

The evolution of operations of U.S. firms within the European Common Market provides a useful illustration of this thesis. It is generally recognized that these companies have moved more quickly toward capitalizing on the economic unification of the area than the companies rooted in individual European countries. With their capacity for structuring operations on a global basis, the multinational firms have more readily made changes in such areas as rationalization of production facilities to benefit from the lowering of trade barriers among countries. The complexity of the process of moving toward unification is brought out vividly in Vern

Terpstra's detailed study of operations of 25 U.S. companies made in the mid-1960s.[19] To varying degrees fragmenting influences have held back the process, especially in distribution and in many aspects of consumer goods operations. But the main thrust is undeniably in the direction of unification strategies. The more effective approach to unification by the multinational firms has regrettably stirred the resentment of local European firms and some of their governments. But if the basic objectives of the EEC are accepted as representative of *European interest,* as distinguished from *national interest* of the component countries, then the multinational firms appear to be serving that interest best by pursuing the unification strategy vigorously. And it would seem quite reasonable to project this line of analysis to a world perspective by proposing that a global unification strategy tends to best serve *world interest.*

SUMMARY

By way of concluding this chapter, it will be well to reexamine the issue which has been the focus of the discussion—fragmentation versus unification. In what ways is this a useful component of a conceptual framework for international business?

The point of departure for the issue was the diversity of national environments to which the multinational firm must relate itself. As compared to the relative homogeneity of parent-country conditions or the unidirectional adjustments in a bicountry relationship, this multiplicity of country characteristics is clearly a distinctive feature of the environment of the multinational firm. That the diversity exerts influences in the direction of fragmentation of corporate structure and activities against certain unifying influences in the corporate nature and objectives seems equally noncontroversial.

The utility of the unification concept has been considered at two levels. First, in a number of specific issues (product policy, logistic planning, distribution of R & D work, financial flows, operating methods, and ownership) it has been shown to be a convenient way of thinking about alternative strategies on a global basis. Second,

[19] Vern Terpstra, *American Marketing in the Common Market,* Frederick A. Praeger, Inc., New York, 1967.

it appears to have meaning in terms of overall corporate strategy. This conclusion may be argued from one direction by the interrelation of unification or fragmentation strategies in specific issues, for example, the interdependence of product policies, logistic plans, and ownership structure. In the final sections of the chapter, some reflections were advanced, suggesting that the multinational corporation was basically a unifying institution in world society and that the performance of its primary roles would seem to call for a general strategy of unification. It must be admitted in conclusion that the conceptual framework in this chapter is fuzzier than in the main themes of the preceding chapters. The difficulties lie in both the ill-defined environmental forces to which strategies must be directed and the diversity of the components of the strategies involved. Thus it seems likely that this piece of the conceptual framework may be subject to substantial revision as the problems to which it is addressed clarify. However, as a useful tool to facilitate analysis of issues currently significant in formulation of strategies in multinational firms, it seems of sufficient validity and utility to be incorporated in this book.

Chapter Six
Organization and Administration

Organization and administration can be looked at in two ways in our conceptual analysis of the multinational corporation. First, they are one facet of the strategy framework we have been examining; and, second, they provide the means for implementing the strategic objectives and policies. The general nature of the first approach has already been suggested in the previous chapters: organizational and administrative skills are among the key resources which the corporation may attempt to transmit; the question of conformity or change is ever present in determining organization and administrative systems in host societies; nationalism and national interests are intimately associated with the people involved in overseas operations; and the issue of unification versus fragmentation appears prominently in determining the structure of people and administrative systems of a worldwide enterprise. In the present chapter, these elements must be considered, for they lie behind many of the distinguishing characteristics of the tasks which the organization and administration of the multinational firm must accomplish. But we must also give full attention to the second approach emphasizing the effectiveness of the organizational and administrative structure in accomplishing the corporate tasks.

The conceptual framework for this analysis is a blend of the processes and strategic patterns already developed and of the effects of the intersection of organizational and administrative processes by national borders. The former establish the main lines of the firm's objectives in international operations—the transmission of resources in which it has comparative advantages, the introduction of feasible innovations in host societies, the counteraction of adverse nationalism and national interest forces by sound application of accommodation and power strategies, and capitalizing so far as practical upon the advantages of its global character. The latter inject into the organization and administrative problems of any large-scale endeavor additional complications arising from the involvement of people of different nationalities located in many countries.

Figure 6.1 summarizes the key components of the conceptual framework. Reference will be made to it throughout the chapter. It describes schematically the organization of a typical multinational firm. The triangles at the top and bottom indicate the structures of the parent company and a subsidiary. As indicated by the S_2 and S_3 notations, there are a number of other subsidiaries. Supervision of the subsidiary in this illustration rests with an individual in the home office located at the bottom of the top triangle. Behind him

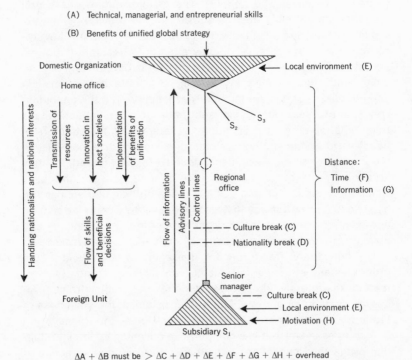

$\Delta A + \Delta B$ must be $> \Delta C + \Delta D + \Delta E + \Delta F + \Delta G + \Delta H +$ overhead

Figure 6.1 International organization and administration.

spread out a variety of people whose work is in some way related to the activities of the subsidiary. These include staff specialists in the home office, senior executives and staff personnel of the parent company, and a variety of people spread through the domestic organization who run factories making components for export to foreign assembly plants, establish worldwide quality standards, or in some other way affect the subsidiary. As one moves away from the point of the triangle, the intensity of the involvement of each individual with the subsidiary declines, but the number of people involved typically increases.

The structure of the subsidiary at the bottom is that of any operating unit, though usually on a relatively smaller scale than that of the domestic units of the parent firm. There is a senior manager in charge and a hierarchy of managers, supervisors, staff people, and workers spreading out below him. Connecting the parent structure and the subsidiary is one line, though as the notation "control lines" suggests, there may be multiple patterns of communication. There may also be some form of intervening regional supervisory unit.

OBJECTIVES

The point of departure of this analysis is the set of objectives indicated on the left-hand side of Figure 6.1. Three of these objectives may be viewed as the constructive inputs from the center of the multinational firm into the foreign units, and they lead to a single general objective for the organization and administrative processes. The three are the transmission of resources, innovation in host societies, and implementation of benefits of unification. If the parent organization is to play an effective role in achievement of these objectives, it must be through the "flow of skills and beneficial decisions," which is set forth as the general objective of the organization and administrative plan.

A basic proposition for the conceptual framework being developed here is that such a flow must exist for the survival of the multinational firm. The assumption underlying this proposition is that unless the parent organization can make contributions to the local organization which permit it to function in a manner superior to an independent local national unit, the international business will not be competitive and therefore will not survive. This proposition seems reasonable in light of the extra weight of the overhead costs and complications which the multinational firm must carry as a competitive handicap. These might be supported for some time simply by superior financial resources, but in the long run the competitive strength of the multinational firm in relation to purely domestic enterprises would appear to require skills and decisions superior to those available locally. The character these superior inputs may assume has been sufficiently described in previous chapters, so they need only be summarized here. In the main they lie in (1) the technological, managerial, and entrepreneurial competence of the parent organization; and (2) the benefits of a unified global strategy including the experience with operation of subsidiaries in other parts of the world which are channeled through the parent organization and the specialization and centralized decision making essential to achievement of the benefits of unification of corporate operations, for example, in logistic planning.

Assuming that the potentials for these benefits are within the capabilities of the international enterprise, the objective of the organizational and administrative structure is to facilitate the flow of the necessary implementing skills and decisions toward the subsidiaries. Along with this is the secondary requirement that there be an adequate return flow of information so that the skills and decisions transmitted toward the field will be appropriate. That is to say, the people in the parent organization who are responsible for overseas activities must have sufficient knowledge of conditions and problems in the subsidiaries if their role is to be performed satisfactorily.

The fourth objective shown in Figure 6.1, handling nationalism and national interests, is an implementing goal. It does not in itself contain substantive contributions to the overseas units, but it is necessary to the successful achievement of the other objectives and to the welfare of the multinational firm. As we noted in Chapter 4, the firm acts as an agent for its parent-country interests, and it has its own set of interests. The maintenance of a sound balance of interests in the continuing processes of international relations requires that these interests be pursued in their varied interactions with the nationalism and national interests of host countries. The organization and administrative plan must therefore provide an effective means for pursuit of interests by the combination of ac-commodation and power strategies discussed in Chapter 4.

These then are the objectives central to international organiza-tion and administration. They establish at the outset a degree of mutual interdependence of the field and parent organizations requiring a certain amount of flow of communications in both di-rections. The flow of communications which may be appropriate obviously will depend upon the nature of the business, being, for example, quite heavy in a high-technology industry in which the coordination among foreign units is great (e.g., the petroleum in-dustry) and fairly small in low-technology industries with highly diversified foreign units.

COMMUNICATIONS GAPS

The problems in achieving these objectives span a range from those which are found in any large, diversified activity to those which are distinctive to the multinational firm stemming from the intersection of its organization and administrative processes by national borders. The determination as to which problems are dis-tinctive is hard to make because, as in many aspects of interna-tional business, the differences are often more of degree than kind. For example, some people might identify the need to adapt control systems to the greater risks of international business (devalua-tions, political change, etc.) as a special administrative problem for international operations. The risks themselves are certainly distinctive and have been considered in earlier chapters, for ex-ample, in the strategy on transmission of capital and in handling nationalism. However, the control systems related to them are, on the whole, similar to those employed in business in general where a range of degrees of risk is encountered. Thus the basic approach to frequency and detail of control measures employed for a subsid-iary in an unstable foreign country will be similar to that for a risky, new product venture in the domestic market. There will of course be many technical differences such as the type of accounting and currency translation methods employed, but this book is not con-cerned with that level of difference.

Accordingly the focus for our conceptual framework must be on the effects of the intersection of national borders on the organization and administrative processes themselves. Within this constraint the problems may be classified as arising from four communication gaps—culture, nationality, environment, and distance. Each of these is also found in domestic organizations, even the second if we note the parallel between nationalism and the we-group feelings of a factory manager toward his plant group and community. But the differences in the degree to which these problems exist in international as distinguished from domestic firms are great enough so that a substantially different conceptual approach to them seems required.

The other distinctive element in international administrative systems is the presence of many currency systems which, for example, inject a distinctly different problem into comparative measurement methods in control systems. This problem is recognized but not dealt with systematically in the analysis which follows. A few words to explain its omission are in order. The presence of many currency systems would be no real problem if the relations between them (i.e., the price levels and the exchange rates) were fixed permanently. The problem stems therefore from the changes in relationships and the uncertainty as to the timing and extent of changes. Designing control systems and other administrative measures suitable to this situation is in large measure an economics-probability problem. As such, it is conceptually quite a different order of subject than the rest of the content of this book. It has not been examined in detail for this reason, with the added consideration that the author does not have the specialized economics-mathematical theory competence to handle it well. Admittedly this leaves out a troublesome problem of administration for the multinational firm. However, as a practical matter in the design of organization and administrative plans, this subject appears as a separate area worked out with reference to its special economics-probability considerations. Thus, its omission does not impair the analysis of the main organization and administrative elements which follows. It simply means that a discrete component of the total problem of the administrative system has been left out of the conceptual framework.

The discussion in this chapter, therefore, focuses on the four types of communication gaps whose characteristics will be outlined in the paragraphs below.

The *cultural gap* stems from the difficulty encountered in communication between people from groups which differ in values, social mores, and other aspects of interpersonal attitudes and relationships. There are of course many differences among people within a single cultural group. This point is brought out clearly in the intensive study of 3,641 managers in fourteen countries conducted by Mason Haire and his associates which showed that "the differences among individuals are about 2½ times as great as the differences among countries." [1] But the people within each general cultural group are accustomed to this range of difference and have learned to communicate with each other despite it. Their communication patterns are guided by the norms and expectations of the group culture, not just by their individual characteristics. Thus two French managers may have quite different personalities, but from long conditioning by their cultures they will have acquired sufficient common patterns of communication so that they can communicate with reasonable effectiveness.

The problem for the multinational corporation lies in the need for communication between people from quite different cultural groups who do not have common norms and expectations. The dimensions of the differences between cultural groups have been described by several authors. They range from fairly easily observed features such as language and concepts of time [2] to attitudinal characteristics like job expectations and the degree of trust felt toward other people.[3] Managers whose cultural experiences differ in such dimensions find it quite hard to communicate even in a common language. An idea expressed by a manager which has a particular meaning in his cultural frame of reference may be received into the mind of a man from another culture with quite a different interpretation. The many ramifications and implica-

---

[1] Mason Haire, Edwin E. Ghiselli, and Lyman W. Porter, *Managerial Thinking,* John Wiley & Sons, Inc., New York, 1965, p. 8.

[2] For example, see Edward T. Hall, *The Silent Language,* Doubleday & Company Inc., Garden City, N.Y., 1959, and Edward T. Hall and William F. Whyte, "International Communication," *Human Organization,* Spring, 1960.

[3] For example, see Mason Haire et al., *op. cit.;* and John Fayerweather, *The Executive Overseas,* Syracuse University Press, Syracuse, N.Y., 1959.

tions of these communications difficulties are beyond the scope of this book. It will suffice for our purposes to recognize them as a substantial obstacle distinct from the common problems of communication between different people within a single cultural group.

In addition to the problems of communication due to differences in the content of cultures, further problems arise in many situations due to the attitudes in cultures about communication itself. In the cultures found in Northern Europe and the Anglo-American countries, people are supposed to express their opinions relatively freely and the value systems stress honesty and precision. In many other parts of the world, however, the prevailing attitudes are quite different. People are supposed to speak much less openly, and under many circumstances they are permitted and even encouraged to say things which are misleading or not true. A subordinate in many authoritarian societies, for example, is not expected to say anything critical about his superior. In many situations Orientals and Latin Americans will give affirmative responses to requests simply to be agreeable without necessarily intending to fulfill the request. These patterns of miscommunication or lack of communication are frequently aggravated in relations with foreigners by emotions arising from insecurity, nationalism, and pride, which are described in my research study of relations between U.S. and Mexican managers.[4] As a result, the international executive is often confronted with a facade which conveys an incomplete and often deceptive picture of the true thinking of the foreigner with whom he is attempting to communicate.

The cultural gap in the full organizational span of an international enterprise is very great indeed, for example, that between a U.S. parent corporation treasurer and a Japanese laborer. The full gap is rarely encountered between two individuals, however. Typically it is bridged by a series of individuals who have to a degree made an adjustment to those in organizational proximity to them so that there are a number of moderate gaps to be bridged rather than a single large one. The chief bridging process is usually accomplished by the third-culture group described in Chapter 4, composed of parent-country nationals who have become quite

[4] Fayerweather, *op. cit.*, pp. 145–162.

familiar with foreign cultures and local nationals who have become accustomed to foreigners. However, even among such individuals the basic cultural differences exist, so the cultural gap remains an important obstacle to communication in the multinational firm.

The *nationality gap* tends to be more clear-cut than the cultural differences. There may be a few unusual individuals who are capable of a binational or nonnational outlook. Most people in an organization, however, will fairly clearly identify themselves with a single nation which commands their nationalistic and patriotic loyalties. There are, as we saw in Chapter 4, a substantial number of corporate activities which affect national interest or may arouse nationalistic feelings. At the point in the international organization where nationality changes, there are generally, therefore, opportunities for misunderstandings and disagreements because of the loyalties of managers which impede the functioning of the business. For example, Indian executives who are sympathetic with typical national attitudes are likely to disagree with their U.S. management associates in the degree to which they should press against their government for scarce foreign exchange for repatriation of profits or departure from prevailing policies on acceptance of Indian capital in joint ventures. In individual cases, the attitudes of either the multinational parent management or the local nationals may be such that nationality differences are not a problem. The essence of the discussion of the characteristics of the third-culture group was that in many expatriates and local nationals the common interest in industrial objectives leads to subordination of nationalistic feelings. Yet we would be attributing nonhuman qualities to executives if we supposed that they could fully detach themselves from these feelings, and where valid differences in national interests are concerned, they must, if only for practical political reasons, be loyal to the countries of which they are citizens.

Further complicating the communications process are attitudes arising from the psychology of nationalism discussed in Chapter 4. Howard Perlmutter has incorporated these attitudes into a general scheme for multinational organizations.[5] He identifies three

[5] Howard V. Perlmutter, "Social Architectural Problems of the Multinational Firm," *The Quarterly Journal of AIESEC International*, August, 1967, pp. 37–38.

types of attitudes: the *ethnocentric,* the *xenophilic,* and the *geocentric.* The ethonocentric is the aggressive, outward component of traditional nationalism. It describes the manager who is convinced that his ways are the best and should be accepted by others. The opposite side of the coin is the xenophobic reaction against the ways of others which is characteristic of many local nationals confronted by multinational firms. Perlmutter does not use this term, apparently incorporating the attitude into his concept of ethnocentricity in the attitudes of some local executives, i.e., the Frenchman whose resistance to American methods takes the form of vigorous assertion of the superiority of French ways. The xenophilic manager is one who says in effect, "We accept your superiority and our inferiority. We shall do as you say and shall comply with the methods and standards you apply to us." This is a sort of unhealthy, negative nationalism but one which exists among many people, particularly in the less developed regions, who extrapolate their country's inferiority in skills into a general sense of inferiority. Finally, Perlmutter identifies the geocentric manager as one who can take a balanced view of the local national ways, the parent-country viewpoint, and the world-enterprise objectives. The geocentric attitude is essentially similar to a nonnational or internationalist viewpoint, at least so far as emotional response is concerned.

The individuals precisely fitting these stereotypes are rare; but the attitudes themselves in varying mixes are found in all managers, and they clearly complicate communication. A quite common pattern, for example, is a home-office group with a strong ethnocentric bias working with local nationals in subsidiaries who show a mixture of xenophilic and xenophobic reactions. The former are so sure of the merit of their own ways that they regularly issue orders, advice, etc., which are inappropriate to the foreign situations. The latter alternate between passive acceptance of what they assume to be sound communications from the all-wise industrial masters and resistance, either explicit or of a submerged emotional nature, to the overwhelming, unsympathetic outsiders. As managements have acquired experience, they have learned to reduce these problems. Thus, in the more sophisticated organizations, careful attention minimizes the communications problems. However, this "careful attention" is in itself an added cost which the communications system must bear in terms of skills required of managers and of time and effort.

The *environmental gap* emanates both from substantive differences and limitations in human psychology. It pertains especially to the problems of individuals in one location attempting to make decisions which are sound for other locations—most frequently the problem of the man in the home office with a responsibility for decisions affecting field operations. The substantive gap involves the acquisition of adequate information about a foreign environment. Even when substantial information has been gathered, however, there remains a psychological difficulty for the individual attempting to project his thinking into a foreign situation while being immediately surrounded by his local culture which is typically his natural environment to which he is most fully adjusted. It is extremely difficult under such circumstances to switch in the proper variables so that the decision making within the individual's mind incorporates all relevant aspects of the foreign environment.

Consider, for example, the problem of an international market-planning manager in Cleveland who is asked to evaluate a proposed program for introduction of a consumer product in Japan. He may well have visited Japan and even have lived abroad for a period, though the odds are it will have been in some other country. The program he is reviewing will be based on a variety of assumptions about buying power, reactions to advertising copy, and the like. There may be some evidence to back up these assumptions, but it will be incomplete; so, much depends on subjective impressions and interpretations. People on the spot will have gained part of their evidence from observations in store visits, reading newspapers, and assorted sources which they cannot readily convey in a report to the man in Cleveland. So he starts his review with an incomplete environmental picture. As he thinks, ideally he should be projecting himself into the Japanese home and the mind of the Japanese buyer, filling in gaps and making relevant interpretations. But all along the way he will, unless he is an exceptional person, unconsciously find bits of the Cleveland environment intruding in answering such questions as: How much benefit will we gain from brand association with our other products? How much influence will the children have on the parents' decision? He may be able to fight off the natural intrusion of the influence of the local environment, but the necessity for effort to fight it off is in itself an impediment to his effectiveness.

Distance taken in conjunction with the limitations of our current communications media causes both *time* impediments and obstructions to the *flow of information.* The time factor would appear to be a minor concern in an age of jet travel and communication satellites. In fact, however, the limitations on available personnel and the problems of communication by various media do result in a substantial addition to the time required to achieve communication in an international structure as compared to a domestic one. Likewise, although it should be possible to communicate information just as fully from Australia to New York as from Kansas to New York, in fact, the adequacy of information flow in the international organization generally appears to be less effective than domestically. Perhaps the problem lies as much in the greater diversity among units in the international structure requiring greater flow of information if people at each end of the transmission process are to be adequately informed. But in any case it is harder to achieve the flow when it must be accomplished over substantial distances.

The equation at the bottom of Figure 6.1 is a way of summarizing the significance of all the factors affecting international organization and administration. The underlying assumption of the equation is the same as that with which this section started— namely, that unless the multinational firm provides inputs which are superior to those of local firms, it will not survive. The equation spells this out saying, in effect, that the incremental gains favoring the multinational firm from greater technological, managerial, and entrepreneurial skills, and the benefits of unification with other components of the multinational structure must be greater than the incremental disadvantages arising from the obstacles to communication in the culture gap, the nationality gap, the environmental gap, and the time and information-flow problems arising from the distance gap, along with the possible lower motivation of hired managers in foreign units as compared with independent local entrepreneurs, and the cost of the overhead in the parent-organization structure. The last two elements are not peculiar to an international business as they are found in any large enterprise in competition with smaller independent units, but they are included here to complete the equation. Obviously it is impossible to insert figures in such an equation, but it is a helpful way of looking at the basic problem of the multinational organization. Essentially the problem lies in optimizing the input increments and minimizing the obstacles to communications and other disadvantages.

ORGANIZATIONAL AND ADMINISTRATIVE PLAN

We have now the main components of the conceptual framework within which the organizational and administrative plan of the multinational firm must be constructed. First, there are the objectives—the three positive, substantive goals of transmission of resources, innovation in host societies, and achieving benefits of unification strategies leading to the general goal of effective inputs of skills and beneficial decisions from the parent to the subsidiaries and the fourth, implementing goal of handling the interaction of interests in the cross-border processes. Second, there are the communications gaps attributable to culture, nationality, environment, and distance. The overall requirement then is to maximize the achievement of the former and minimize the effect of the latter. We may now proceed to consider the application of this framework to the specific problems in the complex and never-ending evolution of the organization and administrative system of a multinational firm. This evolution requires many decisions, and because of the limitations of environment, company characteristics, and individuals, it typically involves many compromises which optimize results for a reasonable term of operation rather than fit any conceptual criteria in ideal form. Recognizing these limitations on any discussion of the subject, we can sort out a few main decision areas and consider the lines of thinking which will best fit our conceptual framework. These issues will be considered under three main headings: worldwide organizational and administrative system, management within foreign units, and managerial personnel.

WORLDWIDE ORGANIZATIONAL
AND ADMINISTRATIVE SYSTEM

The development of a worldwide organizational and administrative system is essentially a total job, all parts of which must be integrated. In the process of thinking through the total system, however, it is practical to consider some phases separately, of which four are most significant here: relation of international units to the rest of the corporate structure, delegation of authority, control system, and supervision methods.

The interrelation of the components of the corporate structure has been the subject of considerable discussion in recent years, with growing attention to the so-called global organization. There is a traditional pattern in the evolution of international firms starting with a small export section, often under domestic marketing, progressing by degrees to a sizable international division with substantial autonomy in managing overseas production and sales. A few firms have now adopted the global concept in which the full top management of the parent organization becomes intimately involved with international business. In the typical larger firm this means that each of the corporate staff sections (personnel, controller, etc.) assumes international responsibilities and that each of several product divisions maintains its own overseas activities.

Although there are several variations in the specific application of this concept in companies, the approach at General Electric Company is illustrative.[6] For many years GE's international operations were segregated from the rest of the company with two country units—Canada and Italy—and two comprehensive units—one for manufacturing subsidiaries and one for export and other operations—all under a corporate vice president. Domestic operations were divided among nearly 100 product divisions, each functioning as a profit center with full production and marketing responsibility. They provided products for export and some assistance in foreign manufacturing but were not directly responsible for overseas operations. There was also a corporate services organization which provided support for domestic product divisions in market research, personnel, etc., but the international group had its own service staff. In 1964, the company was reorganized with *primary* or *supporting* responsibility for the worldwide operations assigned to the product divisions while the corporate services organization added the international aspect to their staff role in various functional fields. IGE continued to handle exports. Other mea-

---

[6] *Organizing for Worldwide Operations,* Business International, New York, 1965, pp. 15–20.

sures to provide international coordination were established, but the main responsibility for serving international markets had been shifted from the segregated international group to the parent product divisions.

A study in 1966 by Enid Lovell of The National Industrial Conference Board showed that only 5 percent of a sample of 100 companies had adopted the global approach. Although 33 percent foresaw a future shift in that direction, some 23 percent expected a shift to greater autonomy for their international divisions.[7] Thus it is by no means clear that the global approach is the ultimate idea, but it is a prominent alternative.

Referring back to Figure 6.1, the global structure has apparent advantages in maximizing the inputs of corporate capabilities, bringing many people in the parent organization closer to the overseas activities. For example, a company may have three or four factories in France, each producing different products; and the global organization would result in each of these being directly tied to parent units with similar product interests and given ready access to a broad band of staff experts in the total corporate structure. By contrast, in the traditional international division structure, such as Figure 6.1 embodies, communication with the parent organization would be funneled through an international division with a smaller staff and all of the attendant limitations in screening of information flow. The global approach should also maximize the benefits from unification by assuring that key decisions are made by men responsible for both domestic and foreign activities.

Yet another advantage lies in the motivations provided for the product divisions to put their best efforts and personnel into the overseas operations. If product X is manufactured abroad under a separate international division, the managers of product X operations in the United States will have less incentive to assign their better production experts to overseas factories than if they have direct profit responsibility for the factories.

On the other hand, the global structure raises real questions as to whether the incremental disadvantages of the communication process are increased unduly, particularly with respect to the cul-

[7] Enid Baird Lovell, *The Changing Role of the International Executive*, National Industrial Conference Board, New York, 1965, pp. 5, 172.

tural and environment gaps. The international division is a device for organizational specialization bringing together individuals with special aptitudes and skills in understanding foreign environments and communicating across cultural and nationality gaps. In the global organization many parent-company personnel with substantially less competence in these communication skills are expected to deal with overseas personnel, and it is quite possible that the lower level of communication achieved would substantially offset any gains from having their capabilities readily available to the overseas personnel. Likewise, in situations such as that cited above where a company has two or more operations in a country, there is a need for unification on a geographic basis as well as on a product basis. The managers of three factories in France, for example, even though they make different products, will have much to gain by exchanging information and coordinating their approaches to labor relations. Undoubtedly there will be benefits from substantial cooperation in financial affairs—dealings with banks, balancing of surplus funds in one unit against needs in another, and so forth.

The advantages of both approaches are sufficiently persuasive so that a clear-cut decision in favor of one or the other is rarely appropriate. Both Lovell's NICB study and a more selective analysis of a few progressive firms by Clee and Sachtjen indicate that most thoughtful managements seek some compromise providing the benefits of both.[8] Even where there is a quite strong international division, the top corporate executives and staff groups take an active part in major strategic decisions, and informal lines of communication are established from foreign to domestic units to assure rapid flows of information, for example, on technical developments. Likewise, where the global approach has been followed in giving worldwide responsibility to several product divisions, international specialists are found individually and in groups throughout the organization to provide expert knowledge and communication skill. Thus in one way or another provision is made to apply, as needed, both competence and collective decision making along three dimensions: product, function, and geography.

[8] Lovell, op. cit., pp. 8–16; and Gilbert H. Clee and Wilbur M. Sachtjen. "Organizing a World-wide Business," Harvard Business Review, November–December, 1964, pp. 55–67.

In the reorganization of General Electric cited above, several such provisions were made: (1) area organizations (e.g., Latin America) were set up to preserve regional expertise and promote relations among the various GE operating units and local governments in each area; (2) the area division general managers could take charge of operation of foreign units in cases where a product division did not yet have sufficient international skill to run them or the units related back to several product divisions; (3) an international business-development organization was established to facilitate coordinated and expert planning for new efforts overseas; and (4) overseas business-integration councils were established at both the senior corporate officer level and at the area level to act as an information exchange and to help prevent duplication of efforts.

All of this suggests three general guidelines for the relationship of domestic, international, and senior corporate organization.

1 The organization should be so structured that planning and decision making on each aspect of operations may be done by people with the breadth of functional, geographic, and/or product responsibility necessary to realize the potentials for unified strategy present in that aspect.
2 The channels for the flow of important or recurring decisions and information should be as direct and short as possible.
3 Individuals with expert international knowledge and competence in overcoming the obstacles to international communication should be readily available within the organization to be utilized wherever their capacities are needed.

When these guidelines along with more general principles such as establishing unity of line responsibility are combined, a number of conflicts are immediately apparent. This leads then to a further observation which Lovell's study emphasizes—namely, that complexity and flexibility are essential characteristics of an effective multinational organization:

> Taken alone, the internal structure of the international unit may give the impression of fairly discrete divisional assignments, with a fixed line of command within each division. But viewed in perspective, as part of a "going" company organization, one discovers a web of liaison, dotted

line, and committee relationships that cut across the formal organization structure and provide the communicating and coordinating links that make it a flexible, three-dimensional management pattern for the company in question.[9]

The question of *delegation* of authority in organizations is one upon which there is now a massive body of basic thought all of which is applicable to international operations. Its application is substantially complicated, however, by the factors shown in Figure 6.1. The achievement of the main forms of inputs from the parent firm generally requires substantial retention of authority by the home organization. This is clearly so for the benefits of a *unified corporate strategy* in, for example, logistic plans and product policies. Hopefully, the foreign units will participate with a cooperative sense of self-benefit in this process, but inevitably the concept of unified global strategy presupposes centralized guidance and decision making. Likewise, centralized decision making often contributes to realization of the economic efficiency benefits of a unified organization. Sometimes it is done to make the superior skills of one individual available to the whole world organization, an expert in operations research methods for example. In others it is found to be more economical to concentrate the skills of a corporation in a single location, avoiding duplication among foreign units.

The transmission of *skills* can be achieved by the flow of information out to the field organization, but in some cases it is more effective to transmit a skill in the form of a decision. For example, pharmaceutical companies generally determine quality standards in the parent-company laboratories rather than trying to train personnel and set up laboratories adequate for determining standards independently in each subsidiary.

On the other hand, the net effect of all the communication obstacles seems to run in favor of maximum delegation to the field, particularly because decision making in the home office frequently is dependent upon the two-way flow of information from the field upward and decisions outward to the operating units. The cultural and nationality obstacles to full transmission, the time lags, and information deficiencies arising from the distance gaps and the

9 Lovell, *op. cit.,* p. 84.

difficulties of achieving sound decision making in view of environmental gaps impeding people in the home office, all detract significantly from the potential advantages in whatever superior capabilities exist in the home office.

Reinforcing these factors which bear on the substantive capacity for decision making are attitudes which affect the capacity of managers to make decisions appropriate to the operational needs of the corporation. The critical element for the multinational corporation in this respect is the nationality gap and the tendency toward ethnocentric viewpoints in both the parent and field units. The ethnocentric manager tends to take a position which supports the things that are important to him, whether it be personal values or the size of the operations under his direction or anything else. For example, in the case cited on page 145 of the firm concerned with rationalizing its manufacturing in EEC, a group of ethnocentric country managers were a major obstacle. Despite what appeared to be preponderant evidence in favor of specializing production of products among the countries, each manager wanted to continue to produce the full range in his own country so as to maintain maximum freedom of action.

Consideration of the nature of these conflicting factors leads naturally to a division of decisions into two groups. Those in which benefits of a unified strategy or the centralized utilization of skills are dominant would generally be made by the central headquarters, whereas others would, so far as possible, be delegated to the foreign units. The resultant system would have much in common with the pattern in any large domestic organization departing mainly in the direction of greater autonomy for the foreign managements. That is, the unification factors are present in more extreme form in a domestic organization (e.g., the need for systematic logistic plans, standardized products, etc., is more important within one country), and so the tendency to centralize decisions is stronger in it. The chief variations in the international structure, therefore, are those evoked by the fragmenting influences.

Inevitably the actual practices of firms vary greatly. E. R. Barlow's study of the practices of a sample of companies showed, for example, a range from companies which exercised tight control over subsidiaries to those which gave almost complete operating freedom.[10] Barlow did find that "practically all the concerns studied established major policy frameworks within which more or less control was granted to the subsidiaries." [11] The major policies included types of products, product quality, key personnel, accounting and financial methods, and expansion of local operations. But in other matters such as sales plans, negotiations with labor, and local pricing decisions, the policies on delegation were quite diverse. Part of this diversity is due to differences in products or other objective characteristics. But to a considerable degree it stems from historical or subjective characteristics and thus does not necessarily represent a well-considered determination as to the most effective balance between centralization versus delegation. Somewhat more illuminating may be the indication that the trend is toward greater centralization. For example, Gordon Miracle, on the basis of an extensive study of international advertising of U.S. firms, reported:

> In the late 1940's and early 1950's, the great majority of large international advertisers followed a policy of decentralization, placing primary responsibility for international advertising in the hands of foreign subsidiaries or local representatives. Domestically oriented corporations which had expanded their sales abroad also climbed on the bandwagon of decentralization. However, by the late 1950's, the trend began to be modified. Although in the 1960's a great deal of decision-making power still is decentralized, some corporations have reintroduced (or retained) a significant amount of centralized management direction and staff guidance.[12]

The pattern of delegation which will be optimum for a particular company will obviously depend upon its unique combination of products, competitive position, personnel, and other characteristics. The key point insofar as our conceptual framework is concerned is the controlling influence of the elements shown in Figure 6.1 and the forces behind them. Thus the essence of the trend toward centralization described by Miracle appears to be the grow-

[10] E. R. Barlow, *Management of Foreign Subsidiaries,* Graduate School of Business Administration, Harvard University, Boston, Mass., 1953, pp. 84–113.

[11] *Ibid.,* pp. 109–110.

[12] Gordon E. Miracle, *Management of International Advertising,* Graduate School of Business Administration, University of Michigan, Ann Arbor, Mich., 1966, p. 13.

ing emphasis on unified marketing plans with attendant efficiency in the use of centralized, high-skill advertising personnel. By the same token, we may expect delegation policies to be influenced strongly by such underlying factors as the decline of skill differentials which would decrease the value of central decision making and the growth of the third culture which would reduce the obstacles to communication and thus facilitate centralization.

As a final note, essentially the type of conclusion reached in Chapters 2 and 5 may be restated. The distinguishing role of the multinational firm lies in the transmission of resources, including skills, and much of its competitive capability compared with local firms lies in the benefits derived from various unified strategies. Both of these characteristics frequently call for stress on centralization. Thus, although the fragmenting influences of local environments along with the major impediments to communication are undeniable arguments for delegation wherever feasible, the heart of the achievement of the flow of skills and beneficial decisions to the foreign units seems to lie in substantial centralization.

The *control* system in the multinational firm is, to a considerable degree, a complement of whatever pattern of delegation is established, both in the information flow it requires and in its psychological impact. The reports required from foreign units must provide the parent organization with whatever information is needed for its decision making. As the foregoing has indicated, this implies an emphasis in the control reports on matters pertaining to major policy decisions in which a unified global strategy is pursued or skills which are centrally concentrated in the parent. For example, in order that it may plan an effective worldwide financial flow system, the parent organization must be well informed as to the profits and financial status of each foreign unit. By the same token, in matters which are delegated to the foreign managements, the need for control reporting is much less and the impediments to communication encourage minimization of reports. There cannot, of course, be no reports on these matters, for delegating is not the same as ignoring. The parent management must to some degree monitor the results of the delegated decisions. This type of question relates to general concepts of control upon which there is much literature; so it is not appropriate to attempt to open up the further ramifications here.

There are, however, two aspects of control which are of special concern in international business. First, there is the problem of adapting controls to the diversity of foreign conditions. Control systems have an inherent bias toward uniformity. In most cases the purpose of control is to provide some comparative measurement as a guide for management—profits are higher or lower, output per man-hour is up or down, and so forth. Within a domestic organization comparative measurements have a certain degree of feasibility derived from uniformity of environmental conditions and internal company characteristics. That is, labor productivity, methods of advertising, etc., will be quite similar throughout the country. A good control system will typically be geared to work close to the limits of this feasibility.

In a worldwide enterprise, however, the fragmenting influences of local environments and certain aspects of global strategy reduce substantially the feasibility of comparative measurement. Workers, consumers, distribution channels, and other factors affecting business performance differ so much that even comparing the results of two apparently similar foreign units in different countries is very difficult. In addition, as was indicated in Chapter 5, the achievement of optimum global results often calls for decisions which favor one foreign unit versus another. For example, a decision to shift profit margins from a production-export country to an importing country, because the latter has lower taxes, will distort any effort at comparative measurement of performance of the two units based on profits.

James Shulman, after surveying the intracorporate pricing experience of a number of companies, observes that the distortion of performance measurements by price manipulation is a serious cause of internal problems. For example, "In one company the United Kingdom division was directed to lower its price to a new French subsidiary so as to improve start-up operating results; but a good deal of ill-feeling was generated when headquarters seemed to forget that the resulting poor performance in the United Kingdom was not at all a reflection of local management failure." [13]

Thus the inherent bias toward uniformity has to be checked and

---

[13] James Shulman, "When the Price Is Wrong—by Design," *The Columbia Journal of World Business,* May–June, 1967, p. 74.

the control system tailored to what may be feasible for each country and for the global system as a whole. Shulman recommends adjustment in the control system to compensate for aberrations resulting from pricing changes, a process which results in effect in two sets of financial performance data—one to maximize actual profits in light of tax, foreign exchange, and other conditions, and one to record as nearly as possible relative operating performances among countries without regard to these environmental conditions.

Second, the control system is a vehicle for helping overcome the obstacles to communication in the transmission of managerial skills to the foreign units. The pattern of performance reports established can do a great deal to educate and motivate overseas units to function according to what the parent organization has found to be effective methods. For example, if a company has found that intensive market planning for each product is sound practice, it may develop the skills of the foreign units along these lines by requiring detailed reports of marketing plans. Some feedback from the home office in response to the reports will doubtless be useful, but the mere fact that the reports have to be prepared will accomplish a substantial portion of the transfer of know-how, which is the desirable objective in this instance. Such use of control reports to foster management objectives is, of course, quite common in domestic organizations, but it has an impersonal and routine character which makes it particularly useful in light of the communications obstacles in the international operations.

Of course, it must be recognized that these very characteristics can be drawbacks if the method is not applied with discrimination because there may be environmental or internal difficulties in its application in one or more foreign units. For example, U.S. companies are frequently anxious to get local national managers to give greater attention to development of subordinate management personnel. In U.S. practice a common device for this purpose is to require formal reports of annual or semiannual conferences between supervisors and subordinates in which the performance of the latter are reviewed and plans for future improvement discussed. Within limits this system is effective in the United States where superior-subordinate relations are relatively open and frank. But in many foreign cultures, concepts of respect and proper content of communication do not permit such full exchanges and even to the extent that they are feasible, there are inhibitions restricting what the supervisor will put on paper about them.

Thus the application of control reports for educational purposes must be tailored both to what education is feasible and what forms of reporting related to it can reasonably be expected. Otherwise, the system can be both ineffective in operational terms and destructive of overseas personnel morale. But this qualification does not detract from the basic idea of using the control system for educational purposes.

The special problem of *supervision* in an international organization is essentially one of personality and personal contact. The requirement of transmission of superior skills and decisions presupposes a positive content in supervisory activity and competence among the supervising executives and their supporting parent staff personnel. Assuming these are present, we find that the critical problems of supervision lie in structural relationships and the difficulties of communication, particularly with respect to the distance, cultural, and nationality gaps.

The structural-relationship problem is intimately associated with the objective of facilitating communication among components of the multinational organization discussed on page 171. Applied to the parent-subsidiary relationship, this objective suggests the desirability of direct contact between the subsidiary and various home office specialists responsible for finance, marketing, personnel, etc. There will typically be one man in the home office who is designated as having line supervisory responsibility for each subsidiary, but he may consistently refer questions to the specialists in the home office and encourage them to communicate directly with the field units.

Maximum use of multiple communication channels is desirable not only to speed the flow of information but also to increase its useful volume. There are both human and structural problems here, which are cited by Wickham Skinner as prime problems from his research in Turkish subsidiaries:

> Both Turks and Americans realized the dependence of the overseas plant on the home office for materials, supplies, information, and technical and management support. In spite of this recognized interdependence, the home office contribution to the Turkish operation *turned out*

to be inadequate. The frequently expressed attitude was: "We'll send those fellows in Turkey whatever they need whenever they need it. All they have to do is ask." However, not only did the foreign managers not always know what to ask for and when to ask, but at many of the home offices the handling of their requests was attempted with one or two people at a so-called "Turkish desk." Naturally, there were problems in obtaining the parts or supplies quickly from the home office and frequent instances of inefficient paper work and inaccuracies in filling orders. The intention to provide the overseas operation with help is not enough unless it is implemented by an organization which is able to cope with the actual needs of the foreign plant.[14]

If all communication must flow through one or two individuals, it is almost certain to be more limited and to be to some degree restricted to what those individuals find of greatest interest. If several people with varied interests have direct contact with foreign units, however, each will broaden the flow of information with respect to his own area. And if these people are directly involved in the communication process, they are more likely to take the initiative in providing help which, as Skinner observes, the foreign units may not request either from ignorance or lack of interest.

Although this structure may result in faster and more complete communications, it can result in excessive attention to details at the expense of concern for the overall performance of the foreign unit. The tendency of each home-office specialist will be to focus on the phase of the foreign unit in his specialty. If given a sense of supervisory responsibility for it, he will regularly seek information, make suggestions, and offer criticisms to the foreign manager concerning that phase. If the foreign-unit manager is subject to this sort of supervision from a half dozen or more home-office specialists, his thoughts are directed away from the business as a whole and toward satisfying the interests of each specialist. Furthermore, as Cameron McKenzie has observed in a perceptive analysis of this problem, his competence may be unsoundly judged, "A clearly inequitable and incongruous situation exists, in that a man who is responsible for the overall operation often is judged primarily on details, by those who are experts in details.[15]

[14] C. Wickham Skinner, "A Test Case in Turkey," *California Management Review,* Spring, 1964, p. 60.

[15] Cameron McKenzie, "Incompetent Foreign Managers?" *Business Horizons,* Spring, 1966, pp. 85–87.

Ideally, therefore, good supervision requires an effective combination of roles. First, the primary supervisory role of the man in the home office responsible for each foreign unit has to be firmly established. Second, the specialists have to acquire skill in performing what might be called a semisupervisory role. That is, they have to be able to perform some part of the transmission of skills and decisions without distorting the perspective of the overseas manager. The characteristics of such a role will, of course, depend a great deal upon the individuals and situations confronting them. However, it implies an ability on the part of the specialist to advise and even to push at times, but with a restraint and recognition of limitation of authority. If this combination of supervisory roles is achieved, it is possible to provide maximum availability of home-office expertise by direct communications. Given the frailties of human nature, it is probably too much to expect full achievement of this ideal. Observations of shortcomings in supervisory systems such as McKenzie cites underscore the strong natural tendencies in the personalities of managers which run against it. Nonetheless, the ideal provides a model toward which supervision planning may usefully be directed.

But even if the supervisory system is well structured, the communications difficulties must be overcome. The distance gap makes it substantially harder to provide personal supervision from the parent to the field units. The frequency of visits must be less. Written communication as a supervisory vehicle is a poor substitute even in domestic operations. It is notably less desirable where cultural and national differences are concerned. An American regional director, for example, supervising a Mexican subsidiary general manager can in a person-to-person discussion immediately pick up misunderstandings and adjust to them. But a misunderstanding conveyed in a letter from a home-office specialist may never be cleared up, or at best it may take the exchange of two or three letters with much attendant annoyance and confusion.

All of this means that prime importance attaches to having as home and regional office supervisors men who are skilled in handling foreign nationals, and a large portion of their work consists of personally visiting and counseling with men in the field. Written communications for supervisory purposes (as distinguished from transmission of decisions and information) have some role, but the supervisors can place relatively little reliance upon them. Referring again to the equation at the bottom of Figure 6.1, the key role of the parent-organization supervisors is to reduce the incremental disadvantage of the culture and nationality gaps with adequate adjustment to the limitations created by the distance gap so that the potentials for inputs of superior skills and decisions on the other side of the equation are increased.

MANAGEMENT WITHIN FOREIGN UNITS

The management of a foreign unit, whether it be a small sales branch or a large manufacturing subsidiary, involves in the first instance the same basic organizational and administrative requirements as any comparable domestic unit—leadership, adequate communication, and all of the other attributes of an integrated organization. The special problems arising from the fact that it is associated with an international enterprise fall into two categories.

First, there is the bundle of things composing the managerial system which are the organizational and administrative aspects of the basic subjects discussed in Chapter 3. That is, there are in any society certain norms of managerial practice just as there are norms of marketing, finance, and so forth. Significant variations from practice in the parent society are found abroad in such matters as authoritarian supervision, paternalism, and nepotism. The problems in this context are essentially the same as those outlined in Chapter 3—namely, to understand the local pattern and then to determine effective responses to it, either conformity or, where it appears appropriate, attempts to change it.

Second, the overseas unit must be considered in the context of the present chapter as a part of the total international structure. Thus, referring again to Figure 6.1, we have a continuation of the flow of skills and decisions down through the foreign-unit organization and similar problems relating to the obstacles to communication. Or stated in another way, the organizational and administrative processes we have been discussing will not be effective if they stop at the level of the senior manager of the foreign unit.

The inputs of superior skills and decisions typically permeate the foreign-unit organization: salesmen take training courses developed in the home office, budgeting procedures developed in the parent company must be adopted by the treasurer, work organization methods from parent-country factories are applied in the production organization, and so forth. The senior manager and other supervisory personnel in the foreign units are therefore continually involved in carrying to effective completion the inward flow process of the parent skills and decisions. Likewise the upward flow of information originates for the most part among individuals spread around the foreign units. For their immediate operational effectiveness, the senior managers of the unit are therefore dependent upon knowledge of business facts, and the attitudes of personnel within the unit and information which they pass on to the home office are largely drawn from others lower in the organization.

The obstacles to communication are related to those shown in Figure 6.1, but with different emphases. For the most part, physical distance is not a significant factor except in large countries like India if one has a geographically spread organization. On the other hand, the problems of the culture and nationality gaps become much more critical at this level of organization. The facilitating influences of the third-culture characteristics of senior expatriate and local managers are much less apparent as we move deeper into foreign-unit organizations. Usually, by the time one reaches the third level in a foreign unit, the individuals are thoroughly representative of their own nationality and culture. That is, the senior accountants, the plant foremen, the sales supervisors, and those in the ranks below them will be typical of their countrymen, relatively little influenced by the parent-company culture or a sense of loyalty to the parent enterprise as such.

Thus the major portion of the cross-cultural and cross-national communication problems must be overcome by the men in the higher management levels of the foreign units. To a considerable extent this is a person-to-person communication problem, for example, the manner in which a U.S.-trained Mexican sales manager induces an area supervisor to be more systematic in the adoption of planning and sales-analysis methods. There are cultural blocks to such changes, which can only be resolved in a long-term, personal-communication process.

But beyond this the managers of foreign units must deal with the general organizational impact of the stream of inputs from the parent organization. The overall pressure for change away from a number of local norms and for a significant degree of conformity with unified international strategies (logistics, advertising, product line, etc.) creates substantial stress within the foreign unit. We are talking here about essentially the same type of organizational problem as is induced by pressure for change in any organization. The individual tendencies to resist change are reinforced by the collective support of a group where a number of people have similar feelings. The special problems for the foreign unit derive from the coincidence and consequent marriage of these collective resistances with nationalism and cultural communication blocks. The basic reaction to the outsider, which was discussed in Chapter 4, comes instinctively to play in the attitudes of the nationals within the organization who see in efforts to change their natural patterns of action not only something to resist because it is personally unnatural but also because it is being inflicted by an outsider, a nonnational.

In sum, the task of the overseas manager is distinguished from that of the purely domestic manager in the conflict generated by the objective of carrying the transmission of parent skills and decisions to full implementation in all parts of the organization against the obstacles to individual communication created by cultural and national feelings, together with reinforcing nationalistic resistance to external forces for control and change. This task can be approached in two directions: first, by reducing the pressure generating inputs and, second, by reducing the organizational resistances.

The former is the least desirable approach, but it is quite common and within limits is justifiable. In the extreme it is synonymous with "going native," the local manager who becomes so much a part of the local culture that he loses sight completely of the parent-organization point of view. Such a man can run a very congenial organization, but he is ineffective in the transmission of skills and decisions from the parent. Although this extreme is inconsistent with the basic objective of achieving constructive inputs from the parent, there is a reasonable case to be made for some moderation of the inputs in the interests of organizational effectiveness. The question here is one of balance. Clearly, if the pressures for change in an organization create too much resistance, the morale of the people may break down. Even though the changes might theoretically have resulted in improved performance, if the resistance to them results in even lower productivity, there will be a net loss. The extent to which application of parent-company skills and decisions should be pushed has therefore to be judged not only in terms of their suitability for the business but of the temper of the local organization.

The organization of work performance in the less developed countries frequently involves questions of this sort. Among the more important skills which multinational firms from the advanced industrial countries may usefully transmit to less developed countries is the efficient organization of specialized, time- and function-coordinated worker efforts. This typically calls for each worker to perform the same function all day, maintaining a pace established by the company. Workers in Europe, the United States, and similar countries have become relatively conditioned to acceptance of such methods. In the less developed countries, however, many workers are still quite new to industrial life, and the degree of commitment to its disciplines is much lower. Thus, even though full application of work organization skills might be most productive in theory, in practice companies often find that workers will respond better and that optimum productivity is achieved if they do not try to go so far. For example, a company assembling radios in Mexico found it best to let workers shift from one position on the assembly line to another. There was some loss in specialization competence, but it was offset by the higher morale of the workers who resisted the monotony of doing one job all day.

The determination of the proper balance should, in principle, be a joint decision of the parent- and foreign-unit managements. In practice, it often turns out that the weight of the decision falls mainly on the overseas manager who is likely to find himself caught in the middle of pressure for acceptance of parent-company inputs and local organization resistance. This is one phase of operations in which the obstacles to communication loom very large. The combined effect of the distance, nationality, culture, and environmental gaps is such that the men in the home office have great difficulty in grasping the dynamic organizational resistances within foreign units. Those from the parent management who travel abroad may be a little better off, but it is still immensely difficult for a man in a couple of weeks to get a real feel for the critical attitudes among lower-management and worker ranks. Thus, the determination of what is a sound balance must really come from the men on the spot.

The second approach, minimization of organizational resistance to parent inputs, calls for maximum accommodation to the local cultural and nationalistic attitudes consistent with achievement of the inputs. That is, as has just been discussed, pursuit of important business objectives will result in unavoidable conflict with some local feelings. But the conflict in these matters can be reduced if management not only does not press against resistance but goes beyond that to positively try to work in accord with the attitudes of the local nationals in other aspects of operations.

To some degree this end may be achieved by policy decisions, the notable example being the promotion of local management personnel to senior positions. This policy has certain limitations, which will be discussed in the next paragraphs. But a concerted, sincere effort by a company to give good opportunities to local personnel can create a favorable attitude in a foreign unit which helps to minimize resistance to other management actions, whereas failure to promote local nationals generally results in greater resistance.

A related policy possibility is the suggestion of Wickham Skinner that the parent nationals assigned abroad be staff specialists, not higher management personnel.[16] On the basis of his research in Turkish subsidiaries of U.S. companies, he concludes that the local nationals are generally capable of handling the higher management assignments, and giving them that responsibility contributes to the overall internal and external effectiveness of the firm. The major skill contributions to be made by the parent organization are competence in running production and other aspects of operations, a conclusion quite consistent with the line of our discussion here. Working on this basis, he feels it is most effective to provide expatriates who are specialists in these skills to work directly in the midst of the operations, rather than trying to bring the skills in through one or more layers of supervisory management, either expatriate or local national. The expatriate specialist appears thus as a staff contributor, a permissive type of role, rather

[16] Skinner, "A Test Case in Turkey," *op. cit.*, pp. 60–64.

than as a supervisor with a controlling, directing role which is offensive to the local nationals. In essence, this approach is designed, therefore, both to make the transmission process more direct and effective and to provide greater scope for local nationals in management and thus improve general morale and reduce resistance.

Although staffing practices of this nature can help, minimizing resistance depends more on personal performance than policies. Each manager in a foreign unit has a wide range of opportunities in which he may either affront or accommodate the cultural and nationalistic feelings of others in the organization. In a large portion of this range he can follow the accommodation path without impairing the transmission of the parent skill and decision inputs. For example, a production manager may have to insist on certain quality and time performance standards which run counter to cultural attitudes to make his factory run well. Achievement in this direction will not, however, be hampered if he does quite a few things which he may regard as undesirable or unnecessary by his own codes but which will be well received by the organization. For example, a high degree of paternalistic concern and involvement in the lives of his subordinates and a strong interest in the history and other elements of the national life of the country can take time and effort which a production-oriented man may regard as unproductive. But they are highly productive in many foreign situations in that they establish a personal rapport which can greatly reduce organizational resistances.

There is considerable similarity between the role of the manager of the multinational firm and that of the technical expert trying to introduce new ways in rural areas of less developed countries. Studies of the latter, undertaken to help technical assistance efforts, have resulted in some guidelines for success for cultural change agents which are quite pertinent to the business manager. For example, in the introductory chapter of *A Casebook of Social Change,* Niehoff [17] identifies the major requirements of the innovator as effective communication, obtaining active participation in the change process and adaptation of the innovation to the local culture. Some of these, such as participation, are almost inevitable

<hr />

[17] Arthur H. Niehoff, *A Casebook of Social Change,* Aldine, Chicago, Ill., 1966.

in the business process. But in the adaptation process and other respects, the main thrust of Niehoff's guidelines is equally meaningful for the business manager. What he does is to dissect each aspect of the process of interaction in the change process and point out for each the ways in which the attitudes of the people whose ways are being changed may be made more receptive.

This approach is one which is readily described but difficult of achievement because of the personality limitations involved. It is not easy to find either local nationals or expatriates who can function in the desirable manner. Again we will deal more fully with the personnel problem in the next section. A few pertinent aspects may be mentioned here, however. We require men who can both press against cultural and nationalistic resistance when that is in order and accommodate to these same attitudes when that is the best course. With the local nationals the problem, most commonly, is that it is hard to find men who will push parent inputs against resistance. But it is not uncommon to find the opposite problem. There are a fair number of local nationals who have made a substantial break with local norms, especially in cultural attitudes affecting management, and who are, to varying degrees, unsympathetic with or even contemptuous of fellow countrymen who still follow tradition. This sort of manager may be unwilling to make accommodations to traditional attitudes of other local nationals on even minor matters and so may aggravate resistance to parent inputs.

But generally the great problems are with the expatriate managers. They are naturally inclined to follow the norms of their parent society. Thus they tend rather readily to pursue the propagation of the inputs of parent skills and decisions. But the accommodation phase generally requires that they break away from their natural patterns. Sometimes it is possible to find individuals who are quite bicultural. For example, Americans who were raised in a foreign country often (though by no means always) are able to function with equal facility according to the cultures of both the United States and the second country. They are the model members of the third culture, and they are best equipped to handle the accommodation process. But for the most part, multinational firms have to make out with people who fall somewhat short of this ideal.

One alternative which suggests itself is finding parent-country nationals whose personalities seem to be consistent with the foreign culture. As was noted earlier, there are in any society a wider range of attitudes than one finds between societies. Thus, for example, there are men with authoritarian attitudes in the United States, even though the cultural norms are quite democratic. But international firms do not, in fact, generally find that this sort of highly selective personality matching is feasible or effective. The trouble is that a good match even on specific points is hard to achieve, and there are so many other attributes involved that a real match is most unlikely to be found. That is, it is not enough just to find a particular American who has an authoritarian attitude, for the patterns of authoritarian management which will be appropriate in a particular foreign country may not come naturally to him. My research in U.S.-Mexican management groups indicated, for example, that there were quite distinct variations in authoritarian styles adopted by U.S. managers, some of which were quite effective and some of which had a negative effect on relations with Mexican subordinates.[18] And probably more important, there will be a host of other cultural characteristics of that country which may not be a part of his natural makeup. Thus, although the idea of finding people whose personalities fit a foreign society is a useful consideration, it is not practical as a fundamental basis for selecting expatriates to handle the accommodation process.

The basic approach of most multinational firms centers around the quest for flexibility. They have found that there are some people who have a facility for adapting to different cultural circumstances. These people are adept at both sensing the patterns of attitudes and action of other societies and modifying their own actions to fit these patterns. Generally such capacities are the result of exposure to varied experience in early life which has forced the individual to develop a degree of adaptability. In extreme form this process is what makes the American who has been raised in another country effective. But there also seem to be additional forces affecting the process, including inherited personality characteristics, the nature of the family situation, and others. This explains why a goodly portion of those raised in two cultures do

[18] John Fayerweather, *The Executive Overseas,* Syracuse University Press, Syracuse, N.Y., 1959, pp. 170–172.

not, in fact, make especially good managers in one or the other of the cultures. If they are not flexible in their ways, they cannot effectively fit into the complex requirements of partially pressing against and partially accommodating to local national attitudes which the multinational firm requires. In general, therefore, the key need is to find individuals who have this capacity for flexibility.

MANAGERIAL PERSONNEL

Questions of selection, training, and assignment of managerial personnel might properly be considered as subheadings under each of the two previous sections. They are treated separately, however, because there is an interplay between their handling and the effects on both the worldwide organization and the foreign units. Policies in this area are important variables in the total process of communication which we have been discussing throughout this chapter. The variables lie primarily in the type of individuals placed at various levels in the communication process and the methods employed to accomplish communication.

The first question is most critically confronted in the selection of personnel for key posts abroad, but it appears in similar form in a number of other decisions. The essential communication problem posed is illustrated by the two possibilities shown in Figure 6.2. In case A the top overseas executive is a local national. It is assumed here that he has characteristic cultural and nationality attitudes so that in the break between him and the home office, we have a substantial piling up of obstacles in the combination of culture, nationality, and distance gaps. In case B we have a parent-country national as a senior man overseas. The communications obstacles are therefore distributed more moderately with the major distance gap between two parent-country nationals and the culture and nationality gaps between a parent-country national and the local nationals below him without the distance impediment.

This, of course, is a greatly simplified presentation of a complex question, so we cannot immediately jump to the conclusion that it is always better to have parent-country nationals heading foreign operations. There are other important considerations including the higher cost of sending the expatriates abroad, their lower level of

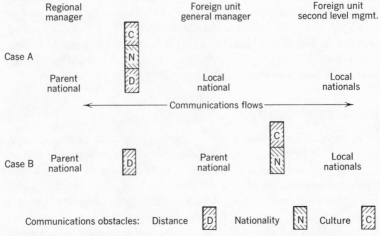

Figure 6.2 Communications obstacles and personnel assignments.

effectiveness in operation in foreign countries, and so forth. Furthermore, it is often possible to find local nationals who are so attuned to the parent culture that the sharp culture break implied in the first illustration is not accurate. A quite common alternative to that suggested above is the assignment of an expatriate in residence in a country or close to a group of countries in an advisory or regional supervisory role who has quite frequent personal contact with local nationals on the spot.

A corollary question is the determination of the type of expatriate to assign to a foreign unit. Even removing the distance obstacle, the expatriate is confronted with a substantial impediment to communication in the combination of culture and nationality gaps. Although the home-office bias may often be toward sending overseas a man who is thoroughly imbued with the parent culture so that he is easy to communicate with, this situation argues for employment of expatriates abroad who are or will become substantially in tune with the local culture. This approach is constrained in most companies by policies of not keeping an expatriate in a single overseas post for an extended period. These policies are soundly based on other logics—for example, the unwillingness of many able men to remain in one country for a long period. But they do mean that it is hard to develop a thorough knowledge of local cultures among expatriates.

As in many matters, such policies must strike a balance among several factors both in general principles and in the realities of specific situations. However, these qualifications notwithstanding, the underlying point remains valid—namely, that the characteristics of individuals at various stages of the communication system have significant bearing on how well the system functions. In the selection and assignment of personnel, therefore, every effort should be made to even out the incidence of communications obstacles and specifically to avoid the pileup of culture, nationality, and distance obstacles at any one stage.

The second question, the methods by which communication is accomplished, has implications both for training and assignments. We have already considered the questions of delegation, control, and supervision, which are also part of this story. The proposition to be considered here is whether it is more effective to transmit parent skills and decisions by training and / or transfer of individuals than by other methods. For example, it may be more effective to bring a local national production manager to the United States for extended periods of training than to attempt to transmit technical know-how through written communications or such guidance as can be given by expatriates sent overseas to work with him. Or it may be that the end can best be accomplished by posting a highly competent expatriate production expert in the foreign unit for extended periods. Clearly this is a very complex question. There are many fundamental aspects to it quite aside from the international implications. For example, the whole question of the role of formal educational programs as distinguished from the training which takes place continuously on the job under effective supervision is relevant to it. And of course much will depend upon the individual circumstances in each situation—the people, the type of industry, and so forth.

But without discounting the importance of these fundamental and specific considerations, we can observe that the nature of the international business situation does have certain general implications which arise from the nature of the obstacles to communication. The cumulative magnitude of the obstacles is such that they will generally provide a significant added argument in each situation in favor of methods which short-circuit some portion of the regular chain of communication. For example, let us suppose a Chicago firm is considering methods of improving the skills of two new production managers—one in Seattle, Washington, and one in Bombay, India. Other things being equal, there would be a stronger argument for bringing the Indian to the Chicago parent-company factory for his training or for sending an American for an extended period to India. Either approach would eliminate the distance gap and the difficulties of difference in environment in communication between U.S. trainers and the Indian. Neither of these problems would be such a great deterrent to attempting to train the man in Seattle by transmission of written material and irregular contact by telephone or periodic personal visits.

SUMMARY

By way of summarizing this chapter, it is well to return to the point of departure with which the analysis of Figure 6.1 started—namely, the proposition that a flow of superior skills and decisions from the parent organization to foreign units was essential for the survival of the multinational firm. The potentials for these superior skills and decisions had already been outlined in the previous chapters. Our concern here has therefore been largely with the structure of the firm and the patterns of activities within it which will facilitate the essential flows. The primary concern has been with the obstacles to communication which distinguish the problems of the multinational firm from purely domestic organizations: the cultural, nationality, environmental, and distance gaps.

Sifting through the many specific aspects of these subjects which have been presented, we find one basic theme: that the organizational and administration plan should be addressed to balancing the requirements of these two main phases of the subject—the flow of superior skills and decisions and the obstacles to communication. Clearly many judgments are involved in the construction of such a plan. In the present operations of international firms one can find ample cases in which skills and decisions are being transmitted which are equal or inferior to those available locally and others in which capabilities to provide superior inputs from the parent organization are not being employed. Likewise, few international executives would argue that they have achieved an optimum method to minimizing the effect of communication obstacles. And achieving a balance between the two is even in theory an immensely difficult task. That is, how does one determine what degree of superiority in skill transmission is necessary to balance the incremental difficulty in the transmission process due to cultural and other obstacles to communication?

These difficulties of execution do not, of course, invalidate the conceptual framework. They do, however, indicate that its practical utility for the time being lies only in the area of general guidance. That is, it provides overall goals and patterns of thinking in constructing organization and administrative plans and particularly in the gradual evolution of those plans in application. The latter is important because, since the difficulties of working out a balance in theory are so great, plans are most likely to be improved through steady evolution in practice. A sense of the direction in which many small increments of evolution should be pointed would seem at this stage of our knowledge, therefore, to be very useful. Furthermore, it is apparent that the differences among nations, lying behind each of the components of Figure 6.1, are constantly changing so that, even as some degree of success is achieved in an organization and administrative plan, environmental factors will require that it be constantly changing if an effective balance in useful flows of superior skills and decisions and minimization of obstacles to communications is to be maintained.

SUPPLEMENTARY READINGS

The following books and articles are suggested as especially pertinent supplements to the ideas advanced in each chapter of this book. Readers seeking further sources will find it helpful to consult the compilation of references in Charles F. Stewart and George B. Simmons (eds.), *A Bibliography of International Business,* Columbia University Press, New York, 1964, and the quarterly bibliographic service, *The International Executive,* Hastings-on-Hudson, N.Y.

Chapter 2
International Transmission of Resources

Gabriel, Peter P.: *The International Transfer of Corporate Skills,* Division of Research, Harvard Business School, Boston, Mass., 1967.

Gruber, William, Dileep Mehta, and Raymond Vernon: "The R & D Factor in International Trade and International Investment of United States Industries," *The Journal of Political Economy,* February, 1967, pp. 20–38.

Kapoor, Ashok: "Foreign Collaborations in India: Problems and Prospects," *IDEA,* Summer, 1966, pp. 213–258, and Fall, 1966, pp. 349–387.

Lary, Hal B.: "Trade of the LDC's," *Columbia Journal of World Business,* Summer, 1966, pp. 66–82.

Polk, Judd, Irene W. Meister, and Lawrence A. Veit: *U.S. Production Abroad and the Balance of Payments,* National Industrial Conference Board, New York, 1966.

Robinson, Richard D.: *International Management,* Holt, Rinehart and Winston, Inc., New York, 1967, pp. 1–56.

Yoshino, Michael Y.: "Administrative Attitudes and Relationships in a Foreign Culture," *MSU Business Topics,* Winter, 1968, pp. 59–66.

Chapter 3
Relations with Host Societies

Arensberg, Conrad, and Arthur H. Niehoff: *Introducing Social Change,* Aldine, Chicago, 1964.

Burger, Henry G.: "Syncretism: An Acculturative Accelerator," *Human Organization,* Summer, 1966, pp. 103–115.

Farmer, Richard N., and Barry M. Richman: *International Business: An Operational Theory,* Richard D. Irwin, Inc., Homewood, Ill., 1966.

Fayerweather, John: *International Marketing,* Prentice-Hall, Inc., Englewood Cliffs, N.J., 1964.

Lee, James A.: "Cultural Analysis in Overseas Operations," *Harvard Business Review,* March–April, 1966, pp. 106–114.

Thorelli, Hans B.: "The Multinational Corporation as a Change Agent," *The Southern Journal of Business,* July, 1966, pp. 1–9.

Chapter 4
Conflicts with Nationalism
and National Interests

Fayerweather, John: "19th Century Idealism and 20th Century Realism," *Columbia Journal of World Business,* Winter, 1966, pp. 77–86.

Gabriel, Peter P.: "Investment in the LDC," *Columbia Journal of World Business,* Summer, 1966, pp. 109–120.

Johnstone, Allan W.: *United States Direct Investment in France,* The M.I.T. Press, Cambridge, Mass., 1965.

Kidron, Michael: *Foreign Investments in India,* Oxford University Press, Fair Lawn, N.J., 1965.

McMillan, Claude, Jr., Richard F. Gonzales, and Leo G. Erickson: *International Enterprise in a Developing Economy,* The Michigan State University Press, East Lansing, Mich., 1964.

Robinson, Richard D.: *International Business Policy,* Holt, Rinehart and Winston, Inc., New York, 1964, pp. 1–224.

————: *International Management,* Holt, Rinehart and Winston, Inc., New York, 1967, pp. 86–100.

Safarian, A. E.: *Foreign Ownership of Canadian Industry,* McGraw-Hill Book Company, New York, 1966.

Chapter 5
The Global Business Strategy

Clee, Gilbert H.: "Guidelines for Global Business," *Columbia Journal of World Business,* Winter, 1966, pp. 97–106.

Fayerweather, John: *International Marketing,* Prentice-Hall, Inc., Englewood Cliffs, N.J., pp. 49–61.

Gates, Theodore R., and Fabian Linden: *Costs and Competition: American Experience Abroad,* National Industrial Conference Board, New York, 1961.

O'Connell, Dennis J., and John J. Benson: " 'Sourcing' Abroad for Domestic Profit," *Harvard Business Review*, March–April, 1963, pp. 87–94.

Robinson, Richard D.: *International Business Policy*, Holt, Rinehart and Winston, Inc., New York, 1964, pp. 147–191.

Shulman, James: "When the Price Is Wrong—by Design," *Columbia Journal of World Business*, May–June, 1967, pp. 69–76.

Solving International Pricing Problems, Business International, New York, 1966.

Terpstra, Vern: *American Marketing in the Common Market*, Frederick A. Praeger, Inc., New York, 1967.

————, Michael Y. Yoshino, and A. A. Sherbini: *Comparative Analysis for International Marketing*, Allyn and Bacon, Inc., Boston, 1967.

Valtz, Robert C. K.: "The Case of the Multiplant Manufacturer," *Harvard Business Review*, March–April, 1964, pp. 12–30.

Zenoff, David: "Profitable, Fast Growing, but Still the Stepchild," *Columbia Journal of World Business*, July–August, 1967, pp. 51–58.

Chapter 6
Organization and Administration

Aharoni, Yair: *The Foreign Investment Decision Process*, Division of Research, Harvard Business School, Boston, Mass., 1966.

Barlow, E. R.: *Management of Foreign Manufacturing Subsidiaries*, Division of Research, Harvard Business School, Boston, Mass., 1953.

Bryson, George D.: *American Management Abroad*, Harper & Row, Publishers, Incorporated, New York, 1961.

————: *Profits from Abroad*, McGraw-Hill Book Company, New York, 1964.

Clee, Gilbert H., and Alfred di Scipio: "Creating a World Enterprise," *Harvard Business Review*, November–December, 1959, pp. 77–89.

———— and Wilbur M. Sachtjen: "Organizing a Worldwide Business," *Harvard Business Review*, November–December, 1964, pp. 55–67.

Fayerweather, John: *The Executive Overseas*, Syracuse University Press, Syracuse, N.Y., 1959.

Haire, Mason, Edwin E. Ghiselli, and Lyman W. Porter: *Managerial Thinking,* John Wiley & Sons, Inc., New York, 1966.

Hall, Edward T.: *The Silent Language,* Doubleday & Company, Inc., Garden City, N.Y., 1959.

———— and William Foote Whyte: "Intercultural Communication: A Guide for Men of Action," *Human Organization,* Spring, 1960, pp. 5–12.

Lovell, Enid Baird: *The Changing Role of the International Executive,* National Industrial Conference Board, New York, 1966.

McKenzie, Cameron: "Incompetent Foreign Managers?" *Business Horizons,* Spring, 1966, pp. 83–90.

Perlmutter, Howard V.: "Social Architectural Problems of the Multinational Firm," *The Quarterly Journal of AIESEC International,* August, 1967, pp. 33–44.

Pryor, Millard H., Jr.: "Planning a Worldwide Business," *Harvard Business Review,* January–February, 1965, pp. 130–139.

Robinson, Richard D.: *International Management,* Holt, Rinehart and Winston, Inc., New York, 1967, pp. 71–85, 148–161.

Simmonds, Kenneth: "Multinational? Well, Not Quite," *Columbia Journal of World Business,* Fall, 1966, pp. 115–122.

Skinner, C. Wickham: "A Test Case in Turkey," *California Management Review,* Spring, 1964, pp. 53–66.

————: "Management of International Production," *Harvard Business Review,* September–October, 1964, pp. 125–136.

————: *American Industry in Developing Economies,* John Wiley & Sons, Inc., New York, 1968.

Stieglitz, Harold: *Organization Structures of International Companies,* National Industrial Conference Board, New York, 1965.

Useem, John, Ruth Useem, and John Donoghue: "Men in the Middle of the Third Culture," *Human Organization,* Fall, 1963, pp. 169–179.

Zwick, Jack: "Is Top Management Really on Top?" *Columbia Journal of World Business,* Winter, 1966, pp. 87–97.

Index

Index